AN **ALTERNATIVE** HISTORY **OF** PITTSBURGH

ED **SIMON**

AN **ALTERNATIVE** HISTORY **OF** **PITTSBURGH**

ED **SIMON**

Belt Publishing

Printed in the United States of America
First edition 2021
1 2 3 4 5 6 7 8 9

ISBN: 978-1-948742-92-4

Belt Publishing
5322 Fleet Avenue
Cleveland, Ohio 44105
www.beltpublishing.com

Cover by David Wilson
Book design by Meredith Pangrace

Massive water
flowing morning and night throughout a city
girded with ninety bridges. Sumptuous-shouldered,
sleek-thighed, obstinate and majestic, unquenchable.
All grip and flood, mighty sucking and deep-rooted grace.
A city of brick and tired wood. Ox and sovereign spirit.
Primitive Pittsburgh. Winter month after month telling
of death. The beauty forcing us as much as harshness.
Our spirits forged in that wilderness, our minds forged
by the heart. Making together a consequence of America.

—Jack Gilbert, "Searching for Pittsburgh"

Pennsylvania's western daughter,
with your tubes of liberty.
Princess of pig iron slaughter,
with your boyfriend Carnegie.

Oh you were stained glass,
you were smoke stacked,
you were laid in cobblestone.
You were trolley car tracked,
And for you the red sky shown.

—Loudon Wainwright III, "Ode to Pittsburgh"

Acknowledgments and Dedication

I've tried to give a sense of this place in all of its beauty and ugliness, its betrayals and its promise. This is, in many ways, a tremendously personal book. When people read it, I hope that they think that it's interesting, that it's engaging, that it's loving, that it's fair. Most of all, I hope that they think that it's the sort of thing that, for better or for worse, could only have been written by a Pittsburgher. It's to the generations of Pittsburghers gone, living, and to come to whom this modest volume is dedicated.

TABLE OF CONTENTS

PART I
Ox and Sovereign Spirit:
Land, People, and Beginnings (c. 300 Million BCE–1799)

PART II
City of Brick and Tired Wood:
Industry, Labor, and Growth (1800–1899)

PART III
A Consequence of America:
Rise, Fall, and Reinvention (1900–)

Afterword:

INTRODUCTION

A friend of mine and I were once at the Squirrel Cage—what locals call that dark, neon cavern on Forbes Avenue with its aura of spilled beer and seventies rock on the jukebox—and we'd decided that "Pittsburgh" was every bit as iconic an American signifier as "Manhattan" or "Hollywood." Those terms mean certain things to people. They have particular connotations, and for good and bad so does Pittsburgh.

The city is indelibly connected to industry, and to all of the exploitative and glorious, filthy and inspiring aspects of that which propelled the American century. Historically it's been a blue-collar town, permeated with a no-bullshit toughness. Pittsburghers like that. Sometimes it's unfairly positioned as a punchline. Pittsburghers like that less. But if the name has meant anything, it's that Pittsburgh is a place where things were once made. There's something important in that.

When I was young, growing up in the city's east end, mills still lined the Monongahela, though Big Steel was then in the process of collapse. My kindergarten was downtown, in the same building where my father worked, and every morning I'd see the mills, not knowing what they were but that they were something important. Now, with some bemusement, having lived over the last decade in New York City, Boston, and now Washington, DC, I watch from afar as Pittsburgh is recast as the next hipster locale, a hidden arts and food city, an unpretentious metropolis valorized on the pages of the *New York Times* Style section.

I say bemusement because unpretentious as Pittsburgh is (and it is that), I hope that we don't let all of the attention go to our heads. Pittsburgh is stranger and more beautiful than any other place that I've lived, so that it never feels quite normal anywhere other than within the Three Rivers. I worry that our Sunday *Times* best might defang us a bit.

Which is why I think of this as an *alternative* history of Pittsburgh. Such a title necessarily begs the question of "Alternative to what?" and I hope that a few words might clarify that intent a bit. In some ways, there will be a conventionality to this narrative: who you expect to be here, will be here. Infernal and blessed Andrew Carnegie, the murderous villain Henry Clay Frick, the alienated oddball Andy Warhol, and Rachel Carson with her bright sensitivities. There will be digressions about steel and coal, considerations of the movements of the French and British in the decades before the Revolution. Nothing is particularly "alternative" regarding such content. In terms of the politics of the piece, any clear reading will show that the book is unabashedly *leftish,* with an affection for workers, rioters, and strikers, but that in and of itself isn't enough to qualify for the adjective that I'm using. Nor should "alternative" be read as some sort of faux punkish conceit, marketing aimed at craft brew enthusiasts and art house cinema fans. Mayor Bill Peduto can encourage hipsters to move to Lawrenceville on his own time.

Rather, I want you to think of "alternative" as being an issue of structure, for though all of the usual suspects are mentioned in these pages, I've not made a claim to completism. Pittsburgh is large and multitudinous, multifaceted, multifractured; it is complex, contradictory, and confusing, so I've tried to craft my own idiosyncratic *Wunderkammer* of representative moments. These pieces of a larger historical landscape are laid out chronologically in their beginnings (albeit not often in their conclusions), which I hope provides an impressionistic sense of what Pittsburgh might mean. Think of it as being less of a history than an assemblage of Rorschach inkblots; not a study or an analysis, but a diary, a dream journal, a wooden shelf packed tight with interesting rocks and shells.

To that end, I've borrowed the favored narrative structure of the great Uruguayan historian and essayist Eduardo Galeano, who in *Open Veins of Latin America* and *Mirrors: Stories of Almost Everyone* (among dozens of others) wrote in a fragmentary, digressive, rhizomatic way, telling histories through a series of related and organized snapshots rather than as some grand, teleological thrust of human progress. As with Galeano, who was Uruguayan through and through, and whose books could have been written by nobody but a Latin American, I believe that nobody but a Pittsburgher could have written the book that you're holding. And also as with Galeano, that means a grappling with not just the light but the dark, not just the sweet but the bitter. This is a book with triumphant things in it, but it is not a book of triumphalism. Some readers looking for Steelers lore (which is in here) or a listing of all the city's beloved native daughters and sons (who still get their cameos) might be disappointed.

What follows are forty short fragments, organized roughly from the earliest to the latest (even while the final content of those sections can range further afield), which attempt to catalog as much as they can the major thematic concerns of Pittsburgh. A single fragment is a monad, reflecting both past and future in a (hopefully) surprising manner, with the ordering of events moving upward and downward like a vein of hidden coal studding the earth's crust in unexpected and unexplored ways. If there is any logic to history, that compendium of one thing after the other, it shouldn't be the teleology of progress, but that every damn thing is connected to every other damn thing. A moldering leaf in a prehistoric marsh is nineteenth-century coal; the river confluence espied by a French explorer becomes the major waterway of American expansion; the site where a steel mill or slag heap once sat is where the newest luxury condominium sits. The set pieces change, but the set stays the same.

Narrative continuity is supplied by the book being divided into thirds, with each section loosely connected to a line from the Jack Gilbert poem which acts as the epigraph of the book. Gilbert was an East Liberty man through and through, and indelibly marked by the city (as we all are, since we can't really leave) so that his "Searching for Pittsburgh" is its own impressionistic history in miniature. The first section, "Ox and Sovereign Spirit," looks at Pittsburgh primeval, from the ancient Pennsylvanian Period of 300 million years ago, when the terrain and resources of the region were established, until the turn of the nineteenth century as the city positioned itself as the first metropolis of the frontier. Throughout this section, it's my intent to give a sense of how much place—rocks and rivers, mountains and valleys—defines the entire tenor of Pittsburgh. The second section, "City of Brick and Tired Wood," tells the story of Pittsburgh's industry throughout the nineteenth century, the ways in which both capital and labor transformed the exploding city. What's conveyed are the ways in which demographics and growth altered Pittsburgh. The final section follows the story into the twentieth century, from Pittsburgh's greatest economic and cultural success through its decline. Appropriately enough, it is titled "A Consequence of America," for if the city's narrative is anything, it's that of the nation in miniature.

Returning to that bar conversation with my friend, part of what Pittsburgh indelibly connotes is an overreaching Americanism, the city's history from frontier settlement (established on Native ground and through violent means), through the Industrial Revolution, the convulsions of labor and capital, and the paradigm shifts of the twentieth century being almost prototypically American. That's been narratively useful, because sometimes circumstance compels me to extend consideration beyond the confines of the actual city proper. Graduate of the Pittsburgh public schools that I am (all twelve years), in personal interactions, I'm often loathe to acknowledge places that aren't actually in the city as being such. When writing a history, however, I must be more ecumenical, since Pittsburgh's story can't be told without also considering Homestead and Johnstown, or for that matter (if we're to fully grapple with the "consequence of America"), Philadelphia and Washington as well.

If I were a bit more hubristic, then I might lean into that claim concerning the consequence of America, because Pittsburgh is arguably the kiln that made America—in all of its canker and gold, all of its filth and glory. If the city is differentiated from other places, it's that the microscopic view of focusing on Pittsburgh still lends itself to a history of the nation of which it is a part. Manhattan is a metonymy for culture and power, Hollywood with entertainment, Washington with government. Pittsburgh is a metonymy for America. If there is one overreaching argument to *An Alternative History of Pittsburgh*, it's nothing more profound than *this is a consequential place, this is an important place, this is a place that matters.*

PART I

OX AND SOVEREIGN SPIRIT

Land, People, and Beginnings

(c. 300 Million BCE–1799)

A Leaf Transformed into Coal

Before there were three rivers, there was an ocean. Before the Monongahela, the Allegheny, and the Ohio, what-would-be Pittsburgh was on the east coast of a long-forgotten continent named Laurasia. By the late Paleozoic, some 300 million years ago, the ocean between Laurasia and the supercontinent Gondwana narrowed, so that the tectonic plates between primordial North America and future Europe pushed up a jagged spine of mountains, peaks that erosion would one day winnow into the pleasant green roll of the Alleghenies and the Appalachians. However, during the Carboniferous Period (named for our most lucrative resource), Pittsburgh was on the edge of a shallow, temperate sea that stretched across the flat basin of the Midwest.

If you could stroll along the silty beaches of Pittsburgh during the close of what geologists call the Pennsylvanian Period, you'd find yourself in the tropics. Temperatures were humid and damp, and the atmosphere was 35 percent oxygen (more than twice as much as today). Across the swampy environs traipsed a number of different creatures: mollusks, bivalve crustaceans, and the ancestors of clams that lined the rocks in the shallow coves of Pittsburgh. Many-tentacled cephalopods and freshwater sharks patrolled the marshes of the Commonwealth, and though decreasing in numbers as they slid toward extinction, the shiny hard bodies of trilobites accumulated in the ponds, creeks, streams, and mangroves. Pleasant-looking *Fedexia,* a two-foot long amphibian appearing like a large salamander, made her home here, and *Hynerpeton* would have waddled from the water to the land with her stubby, amphibious legs while she smiled her broad, froggish grin.

A novel occurrence upon the land, as the earliest reptiles began laying amniotic eggs, their speckled, hard shells making it possible to give birth outside of the water. And because of the oxygen-rich air, which allowed them to more efficiently respirate, arthropods and insects were able to reach gargantuan proportions, including the grotesque *Arthropleura,* centipedes that grew longer than six feet, with smooth eyeballs the size of softballs. They were joined by *Meganeura,* dragonflies that had twice the wingspan of a dove. As the biochemist Nick Lane soberly remarks in *Oxygen: The Molecule that Made the World,* "Gigantism was unusually common in the Carboniferous." During this period there were spiders with two-foot long legs, scorpions three feet long, and newts that reached dimensions of an astounding sixteen feet. *Arthropleura*'s perambulations and *Meganeura*'s swoops, light refracted through the gossamer fabric of her rainbow wings, remind us of the inviolate wisdom of paleogeography, paleontology, and geology—this land is ours, but only for a bit.

Over the eons, silty beaches pressed into sandstone, and further west, the preserved bodies of millions of corals transformed into green limestone, a rich vein to be tapped by miners. Thick-branched, green-palmed fronds reached out of the sun-dappled mangroves that covered Allegheny County, and when they died and fell into the shallow, tepid water, the lack of wood-consuming bacteria (which hadn't evolved yet) ensured that these fibrous plants wouldn't decompose. Instead, they sank into the silty soil like eternal, beautiful corpses, petrifying into statues. In the rock there is evidence of the sublimity of deep history, the foreign country which composes the epochs—palms converted to peat, and peat transformed into rock. From those dead trees, there was a symphony of compression that molded them into black carbon, the bituminous that threads in a vein across the ocean from Canonsburg, Washington County, to Cardiff, Wales.

Mt. Washington, overlooking the skyline of Pittsburgh from the southern bank of the Monongahela, was not there 300 million years ago, but the pressed remains of fern and *Fedexia* have long been entombed there as hard anthracite. Before it was called "Mt. Washington," it was named "Coal Hill" by the English settlers at the forks of the Ohio who noted the rock's presence because the well water was as dusky as it was in Wales and Cornwall. When the first mining operation opened there in 1762, coal was cut from the side of the rock face and transported on horseback into the settlement where it heated winter rooms. By the late nineteenth century, over thirteen million tons of coal were excavated annually. Lane writes that "Coal that was buried in the Carboniferous, and is today dug out and burnt, was nonetheless buried for 300 million years. Its burial helped raise atmospheric oxygen levels throughout this time, just as burning it is lowering them again today."

Arthropleura and *Meganeura* thus have their revenge; their cremation pushing carbon dioxide in our atmosphere up toward untenable levels. Call it a geological irony, as the long-dead remains of creatures we can scarcely imagine facilitate an extinction of our own doing. We transformed their bodies into energy, but they finally made their mortality our own. In *What is Life?*, evolutionary theorist Lynn Margulis wrote that "Life today is autopoietic . . . planetary in scale. A chemical transmutation of sunlight, it exuberantly tries to spread, to outgrow itself. . . . Life transforms itself to meet the contingencies of its changing environment and in doing so changes that environment." Both explanation and cracked hope in that, for life shall ever remain, even if we don't.

British geologist Jan Zalasiewicz, in his poetic *The Planet in a Pebble: A Journey into Earth's Deep History,* ruminates on an individual rock, writing that its "stories are gigantic, and reach realms well beyond human experience, even beyond human imagination." A pebble extends "back to the Earth's formation. . . . Something of the Earth's future, too, may be glimpsed beneath its smooth contours. Battle, murder, and sudden death are there, and ages of serenity too." So it is with a pebble that you might come across while hiking the orange and red thicket of Frick Park on a crisp autumnal day, some small shard of earth having been here in Pittsburgh millions of years before, a resident over the millennia, mute witness to when Pennsylvania glaciers encroached just north of the city, to when this place was on the coast upon a silty beach, to when it was under the ocean. Epics of epochs. Stanzas of strata. There is a lyricism to minerology and a poetics of geology from the distant past to the far future. People die, but pebbles remain.

Geologists have taken to calling our own epoch the "Anthropocene," the age when humanity makes its mark on the world. But in some sense it's an aftershock of the Pennsylvanian, casting its coal upon the ever-warming water from some 300 million years in the deep past. If geology is but poetry in rock, what stanza do we contribute? Perhaps 300 million years hence, there will be just a few centimeters, maybe a foot, of rock shot through with steel, reinforced concrete, and plastic, testifying to the reality that we once existed.

The Pre-Clovis

Known to the local Inuit as *Injaliq,* the Alaskan village of Little Diomede sits on a small island in the midst of the Bering Strait, population 115 (and shrinking). Injaliq is located only 2.5 miles to the west of the town of Imaqliq, which is the most eastern Russian settlement. According to most anthropologists, it is here that the ancestors of America's indigenous population traversed into this hemisphere, when it remained cold enough for much of the world's water to be locked into Arctic glaciers, but temperate enough that Beringia offered ground on which to walk, some 11,000 years ago.

This Paleo-Indian people that migrated from Siberia are known as the Clovis culture, after the town in New Mexico where some of their oldest artifacts are to be found. Despite its distance from New Mexico, it's assumed that this fifty-mile-wide nautical swath separating Alaska from Russia was where the final goodbye kiss between Asia and America happened. Anthropologist Dennis J. Stanford writes in *Across Atlantic Ice: The Origin of America's Clovis Culture* that though many scholars "have long held that the peopling of the Americas was a more complicated issue," the Bering Strait traversal remains a "highly logical hypothesis" that was "quickly adopted by the archeological profession and locked investigators into . . . [a] nearly unshakable notion." But as history is an ever-fickle thing, we're simultaneously haunted and enticed by the exceptions that imply reality is more complicated.

Tracing paleolithic migration is inexact; evidence is transient since buckskin decomposes and stone tools are eroded by creeks and streams. Travel writer Craig Childs reminds us that the "land bridge remains a hypothesis. Though early people are found on both sides, no physical artifacts or sites have been discovered to prove that they crossed through here." The date of arrival is pushed back, challenged by any number of data points. Not least of which is that even though Pittsburgh is 3,682 miles from Little Diomede, it's only twenty-seven miles from Avella, where a farmer named Albert Miller discovered artifacts in a rock shelter that would eventually be dated to 19,000 years ago, anticipating the Clovis people by eight millennia. Not only is the Meadowcroft archeological site the oldest provable inhabitation in North America, *it's the oldest continuously occupied settlement* as well.

Miller's artifacts were discovered while excavating a groundhog hole in 1955, but he wouldn't generate any scholarly interest until 1973, when archeologist James Adovasio agreed to survey the land as part of a project for the University of Pittsburgh. Adovasio surmised that the artifacts were of a different design than those associated with the Clovis, and in the ensuing decades, those arrowheads were joined by the aftermath of firepits, weapons, pottery, and the remains of around 150 plant and animal species, including the staples of corn, squash, and beans. From a cave that served as a seasonal habitation for indigenous hunting parties, Adovasio would find millions of artifacts.

As he recounts in *The First Americans: In Pursuit of Archaeology's Greatest Mystery,* the "people who made these tools were no novices . . . they imported high-quality materials: Kanawa chert from West Virginia, Flint Ridge material from Ohio, Pennsylvania jasper, and Onondaga chart from New York." In the rocks outside of Pittsburgh, Adovasio and Miller found evidence of an advanced, widespread, and forgotten world. Radiocarbon dating allowed Adovasio to conclude just how ancient Meadowcroft was; conclusions that, if they were controversial in the 1970s, have quickly become scholarly consensus. As archeologist David J. Meltzer assures readers in *First Peoples in a New World: Colonizing Ice Age America,* "by all accounts—including those of the site's harshest critics—the work was superb."

Whether those who called Meadowcroft home came from the east or the west and how exactly they're related to subsequent Indian populations is an issue of controversy, however. It is possible that the ancestors of both the Meadowcroft and Clovis peoples came across the Bering Strait over millennia. Or perhaps, as adherents of the contested Solutrean hypothesis hold, the former may have arrived from the east on small rafts and boats linking southern Europe to the Arctic and then to the Western Hemisphere. Another position, Stanford explains, is that of many of the Natives themselves. "Many [Indians] oppose the theory that their ancestors came across a land bridge from Asia—or from anywhere else," Stanford writes. "Their ancestors, they argue, were created in their traditional American homelands; they didn't migrate from another continent," and it's crucial to remember and respect that perspective—when flint and stone chip fail us, there is a wisdom in that.

Despite the ineffability of origins, there is something intimate and personal in climbing down into the rock shelter. Adovasio recalls how at the closest strata, his undergraduates found beer bottles and drug paraphernalia left by bored teenagers. Then they found the trash of the European settlers in this area, the Scots-Irish who arrived in the eighteenth century (and from whom Miller descended). Beneath that, they unearthed the discarded refuse of the Monongahela Indians who made this region their home in what would have been the Middle Ages, and then earlier and earlier groups back to those original people for whom we don't even have a name. But as different as those ages may have been, Adovasio detected an important human unity as well, explaining that "We had come across some twenty levels of prehistoric fireplaces, showing that at this spot for literally thousands of years people had been taking it easy, sitting around the fire, munching." Here, underneath a few meters of collapsed granite and sandstone, humanity had unfolded over the millennia.

The lives of those original, unnamed people who sought shelter at Meadowcroft were inevitably filled with love and fear, sadness and rage, frustration and joy, as surely as anyone else who's occupied this place. The original Pittsburghers, these first Americans, were people after all, and like most of us they lived lives that were to be buried and forgotten.

The Great Peacemaker

There were hungry years on the ribbon of the Allegheny Mountains. Among the Iroquoian people of the Seneca, Cuyahoga, Onondaga, Oneida, and Mohawk, life was defined by famine, pestilence, warfare, and death. Describing the area in *1491: New Revelations of the Americas Before Columbus,* science journalist Charles C. Mann writes that the "Adirondack and Allegheny forests . . . [were] a place of constant violence, and, apparently, intermittent cannibalism." The five tribes had been involved in generations of revenge killings, answering the slaughter of daughters and sons, wives and husbands, mothers and fathers with equivalent punishment, from the confluence of the Ohio to the Finger Lakes. In the frigid winters, the snow was dyed red, and in the baking summers the green leaves dripped with blood, the entirety of Pennsylvania a veritable empire of bleached skulls stripped bare.

A leader of the Onondaga named Tadodaho was responsible for the deaths of the Mohawk chief Hiawatha's daughters. Hiawatha decided that such bloodshed had to end. He would find himself the first disciple of a prophet whom Mann describes as a "shamanic outsider who was born to a virgin girl," emerging somewhere in the traditional region of the Iroquois. Deganawidah, known as the Great Peacemaker, was possibly Onondaga, Mohawk, or Huron, or perhaps born from the very soil itself. His name, however, meaning "Two River Currents Flowing Together," indicates a western Pennsylvanian origin. Hiawatha helped spread the message of Deganawidah, so that the former was the head, the latter the heart; the first the mind, and the second the spirit; the two joined together in the conversion of their people to the Great Code of Peace.

Tadodaho was the last sachem to be converted to the new faith. Hiawatha and Deganawidah explained the utility of alliance to him by demonstrating how easy it was to snap a single arrow in two, but how difficult it was to do when five were bound together. Fearsome as Tadodaho was, Hiawatha's forgiveness toward him was the genesis of the Iroquois Confederation, which was to be centered near modern-day Syracuse, New York (where indeed the capital of the Iroquois remains). What would be Pittsburgh, by the eighteenth century a small Seneca village on the eastern banks of the Allegheny known as Shannnopin, was but one small corner of the Iroquois Empire.

In *An Indigenous Peoples' History of the United States*, Roxanne Dunbar-Ortiz describes the resulting political order inaugurated by Deganawidah and Hiawatha as a "remarkable federal state structure," a system which incorporated "six widely dispersed and unique nations of thousands of agricultural villages and hunting ground from the Great Lakes and the St. Lawrence River to the Atlantic, and as far south as the Carolinas and inland to Pennsylvania." Mann described the Iroquois Confederacy as "the greatest indigenous polity north of the Rio Grande in the two centuries before Columbus, and definitely the greatest in the two centuries after." Based on an eclipse that is central to the tale of Deganawidah, it's possible that the legendary events of the founding of the confederation known as the Haudenosaunee may be as late as 1451 and as early as 1142. If the earlier date is accurate, than Mann makes the observation that the political alliance would, after the Icelandic Althing, be "the second oldest continuously existing representative parliament on earth."

In 117 codicils, Deganawidah's Great Code of Peace specified in exacting detail how the relationship between the five nations was to operate. Fifty sachems from throughout the Iroquois country were to represent the five tribes at occasional longhouse tribunals held near Syracuse; each one of the male chiefs was selected by women who were the leaders of their individual nations. Scholar Barbara Mann (of no relation to Charles) notes in *Iroquoian Women: The Gantowisas* that "men could not consider a charter not sent to them by the women," leading the other Mann to note that the Haudenosaunee could be regarded as "a feminist dream."

All collective decisions had to be unanimous, forcing the Cuyahoga, Mohawk, Onondaga, Oneida, and Seneca into not just an official policy of compromise, but indeed an entire philosophical disposition that prized such unity above all else. Deganawidah's Great Code of Peace was a radical document, arguably more democratic than anything produced in ancient Athens. Its fundamental axiom, conceived some six centuries before the Declaration of Independence, was "That one's as much Master as another, and since Men are all made of the same Clay there should be no Distinction or Superiority among them."

Eighteenth-century observers credited the Haudeno-saunee's democratic spirit. Cherokee colonist James Adair noted that "Their whole constitution breathes nothing but liberty," while the British military officer Robert Rodgers recorded that among the Iroquois, "Every man is free" and nobody "has any right to deprive [anyone] of his freedom." While Europe was mired in despotism, and American colonists projected their utopian dreams of human freedom onto the continent, the Haudenosaunee had been engaged in egalitarian self-governance for the better part of a millennium. Still, a direct line between Syracuse in 1142 and Philadelphia in 1776 (and then again in 1787) seems, as Mann writes, if "Taken literally ... implausible." If not for the very least that the Great Code of Peace is profoundly more egalitarian than the US Constitution.

Mann writes that "the Constitution's emphasis on protecting private property runs contrary to Haudenosaunee traditions of communal ownership." For the Iroquois, the alliance between their nations signified political, social, cultural, and religious emancipation, not just the delineation of how to protect the rights of property owners. Physician and governor of the Province of New York, Cadwallader Colden, noted with admiration in 1749 that the Iroquois had "such absolute notions of Liberty that they allow of no Kind of Superiority of one over another, and banish all Servitude from their Territories." The Haudenosaunee represented the first organized, large-scale, genuine democratic experiment, not in the groves of the Peloponnesus but in the forests that included pre-Colombian Pittsburgh and its environs in the Mid-Atlantic.

Mann writes that American democracy, when imagined in its purest sense, is "pervaded by Indian ideals and images of liberty," that the nation is "infused by the democratic, informal brashness of Native American culture." A risk, no doubt, in that type of language, the possibility of falling into tired (and dangerous) stereotypes about "noble savages." But if we remain focused on what the Haudenosaunee Great Code of Peace said, what we do find is something profound: the existence of a democracy in more than name only, a system promulgated by a prophet who was the first to utter that sacred ideal concerning the equality of all women and men, and who had the political endurance to actually enact it—not on heaven, but on earth.

Land Granted

Held in the Library of Congress are a series of workmanlike paintings titled *The Pageant of a Nation,* composed by the Philadelphia-born artist Jean Leon Gerome Ferris in the late nineteenth century. Ferris meant to illustrate pivotal moments in patriotic history, a stations of the cross for American civil religion. Paintings like *The Mayflower Compact, The First Thanksgiving, Writing the Declaration of Independence,* and *Betsy Ross, 1777* all serve to construct an idealized view of the past, stolid and sober as it is sentimental and sanctimonious. Ferris's depiction of the founding of his own state, *The Birth of Pennsylvania, 1680,* is no different.

Ferris depicts William Penn in the chambers of Charles II at Whitehall, as the king presents to the Quaker the charter for the new province to be named in honor of the latter's father. Charles II is seated on the left, every inch of him the resplendent libertine in heavy yellow coat, framed with cascading, curly chestnut locks and purple-stockinged legs crossed at his shapely calves. The King's retinue is similarly dandyish: frivolous and foppish young men in powdered wigs, buxom ladies twittering amongst each other, an African slave in turban and Maghreb garb. And there, on the right, is Penn, holding the charter for his province. Upon his head is a simple black tricorne, removed not for a king, but for Christ alone.

Historian Alan Taylor writes in *American Colonies: The Settling of North America* that Penn was a "paradoxical man . . . [who] combined an elite status with radical religion." A convert to Quakerism, Penn's powerful father had ironically been an admiral in the English Navy, first in the service of Oliver

Cromwell's interregnum government, and then with Charles II during the Restoration. The elder Penn begrudgingly developed a respect for his son's steadfast faith, and though his son had been imprisoned several times for his prominence within the heretical sect, Charles II had assured the dying admiral that the court would protect Penn upon the elder's passing.

A fortuitous promise, as Charles wished to dispatch with all of these pesky Quakers in England anyway. He had no use for those who refused to acknowledge hierarchy or to doff their caps toward their superiors. And so from Charles's own North American landholdings, the king would carve out 45,000 square miles of land far south of the strict Puritans of New England and far north of the oppressive slaveholders of Virginia, in a land that Penn called "New Wales," but which the monarch christened "Pennsylvania," in honor of the elder Penn's service in the conquering of Jamaica.

Suddenly, the man who'd once scribbled heretical pamphlets in Newgate was in possession of the single largest individual land claim in the entire world. Taylor writes that Penn had "organized the fastest and most efficient colonization in the seventeenth-century English empire." Penn would declaim that "It is a clear and just thing, and my God who has given it to me through many difficulties, will, I believe, bless and make it the seed of a nation." He envisioned a land defined by and rooted in Quakerism's founding principles. An experiment in religious tolerance and freedom in the New World.

But what exactly were the parameters of this new proprietary colony, answerable to neither charter as in Massachusetts nor royal prerogative as in Virginia? On the east it was to be bound by the Delaware River, which was the border with West Jersey. To the north lay the land that had once been New Netherlands, but which had since been forcibly ceded to the Duke of York. To the south were the proprietary holdings of Cecil Calvert, the Catholic Baron Baltimore. Some ambiguity on those parameters led to several skirmishes between the provinces in the coming century, culminating in Cresap's War, when Pennsylvania and Maryland actually went to (smallish) blows, settled only when Charles Mason and Jeremiah Dixon defined that latitude that would mythically solidify the border between North and South.

And what of to the west? Well, of that there was some disagreement, for if the borders in the other three cardinal directions were better defined, the great western interior of the continent, that kingdom of buckskin and acorn stretching onward to an undifferentiated and apocalyptic frontier, was more uncertain. That Penn's landholdings stretched beyond the Susquehanna and into the Allegheny Mountains was at least clear to him, but what exactly it meant to be Pennsylvanian once you'd left the safe environs of the east remains a pertinent question. Especially true, since if Pittsburgh was in Pennsylvania, Pennsylvania was not yet in Pittsburgh.

Traditionally, the French explorer René-Robert Cavelier, Sieur de La Salle is regarded as the first European to arrive at the Iroquois village of Dionde:gâ on the banks of the Allegheny, but more recent research has cast doubt on the accuracy of that claim. The first written description of the land was made by a Virginian trader named Michael Bezallion much later, in 1717. Pittsburgh has always been as liminal as the frontier, its geography as ambiguous as its discovery. Its location is strung between both East and West, and the city is less than a hundred miles north of that famed Mason-Dixon line. In the years before the American Revolution, the headwaters of the Ohio would be claimed by both Pennsylvania and the Royal Colony of Virginia; the site would be contested by both the English and French.

Much of Pittsburgh history is lacunae, as unclear as who once made Meadowcroft their home, or when the Great Peacemaker lived and died. The western frontier has always been as shadowy and mysterious as an errand into the wilderness.

1754

Mass at Fort Duquesne

No lithograph, drawing, or painting exists of the humble chapel which the French consecrated as the Assumption of the Beautiful Virgin at the Belle Riviere on the sandy banks of the waterway which they referred to as the Beautiful River, but which the indigenous called the Ohio. By 1754, the British had already arrived at the forks of the Mississippi's greatest tributary, but their attempt to build Fort Prince George was aborted as French soldiers arrived from Quebec to claim the entire Allegheny River Valley. Here was to be the eastern terminus of the massive empire of New France, what Voltaire had dismissively referred to as "A few acres of snow," but which in reality was the linchpin of Versailles's colonial policy.

Across Canada and the Great Lakes, France built a mercantile empire built on the fur industry, and whose shock troops were the Jesuit and Franciscan missionaries who lived amongst the Natives from the St. Lawrence River to Lake Michigan, and up and down the breadth of the internal continent, while the English still clung to the Atlantic Coast. When the French arrived from the north to easily push the English from their position at the headwaters of the Ohio, they named the new settlement Fort Duquesne in honor of New France's governor-general. Among their first tasks was the construction of that simple Roman Catholic chapel.

On April 17, 1754, a day after their arrival in this new French city, the first Mass would be celebrated. The officiant was a priest in the Recollect Branch of the First Order of St. Francis named Charles Baron, who upon ordination took the name Father Denys Baron in honor of the Montmartre saint who famously picked his own head up after he was decapitated by the Romans. Baron was described by J. E. Wright and Doris S. Corbett in *Pioneer Life* as a figure who "became familiar in the coarse brown habit of the . . . friars, with its cowl and its rope girdle, from which dangled a crucifix." For two years, until he'd be transferred to Ticonderoga, Fr. Baron would minister to the Catholics of Duquesne, an assortment of not just Frenchwomen and men, but of Irish Catholics, English converts, and baptized Lenape and Iroquois. Fr. Baron's notes are still preserved at the Supreme Court of Lower Canada for the District of Montreal, and they present a narrative of daily life in Duquesne, of that comingling of the sacred and profane, which mark our existence.

A year after the first Mass, and Fr. Baron would baptize John Daniel Norment; a few months later and he'd bury a trader who "was killed by the Shawnees while coming to join the Catholics of these parts." Fr. Baron also recorded the welcoming into the Church of "John Baptist Christiguay, Great Chief Iroquois, aged ninety-five years, or thereabout, who being dangerously sick, earnestly desired Holy Baptism." Fr. Baron's interests in the joys and tragedies of life was more than just theological, for as Leland Dewitt Baldwin writes in *Pittsburgh: The Story of a City, 1750–1865* (with just a hint of conjecture), "it was whispered that he had once been a cavalry officer and had become a priest after the death of the girl whom he was to marry." Paradise is not man's to construct on this planet, for death, famine, pestilence, and war shall be things of this world until Judgment Day. As such, Fr. Baron delivered homilies about birth and death, sin and redemption, and as Britain and France slid inextricably toward global conflagration, about war.

Duquesne would be the spark that set aflame the Seven Years' War. Arguably the first world war, the conflict would see battles on three continents. It would stretch from

Monongahela to Mumbai, and a central concern was whether the British or the French would control the interior of the North American continent. According to journalist Maryann Gogniat Eidemiller in an article for the *Pittsburgh Tribune-Review,* following a Mass of Fr. Baron, the commanding officer of Fort Duquesne, Daniel Hyacinthe Liénard de Beaujeu, "stripped off his shirt, painted his chest, strapped on a metal shield of armor and marched out with his men and their Indian allies." He'd be killed in a battle which the French would win (even while they'd lose the war), with Fr. Barron noting that the soldier's death occurred after "having been at confession and [having] performed his devotions the same day." Beaujeu would be buried in the cemetery of Fort Duquesne, which was to be erased by the English, his remains somewhere underneath downtown Pittsburgh.

Fr. Baron's church in the wilderness lacked the sublime gothic beauty of a Notre-Dame or a Chartres, but what did dwell there was faith—faith within the forest, faith among brutality. Appropriate that a Franciscan's mission should be here, in the wild country of a North America that was so fecund; something transcendental about that sort of chapel, there in the woods, even when the leaves and branches would ultimately drip red with French, Indian, and English blood.

General Braddock's Defeat

For sixty-five years, Daniel Boone lived in the ghostly presence of a haunted wood of oak and maple. He became a famed and celebrated frontiersman and explorer, the subject of innumerable articles and penny-dreadful novels while he was still alive, yet he'd forever be preoccupied with one formative day of bloodshed.

In the summer of 1755, Boone and a regiment of Virginians led by the Scotsman General Edward Braddock would cross the Monongahela River in anticipation of conquering Fort Duquesne, only to find themselves attacked by a much smaller column of French Canadians and their Indian allies who would decimate the British and their American soldiers.

The forks of the Ohio were claimed by both England and France, while British colonies also disagreed with their provincial lines at the murky western hinterlands of the map—Virginia reached a high-water mark as far north as the current site of Pittsburgh's East Carson Street. Though Boone was a Pennsylvanian by birth, and eventually a Kentuckian by choice (though the latter was part of Virginia at the time), it was on behalf of Governor Robert Dinwiddie that a twenty-one-year-old Boone served as a wagon driver with Braddock's men. At Monongahela, the British would find themselves in a Thermopylae, cast in the role of the Persians.

Legend said that as a child, Boone shot a panther through the heart the moment before the beast could rear up and attack him; the man who cleared a path deep into the western frontier and became a veritable archetype of manifest destiny. His biographer John Mack Faragher, writing in *Daniel Boone:*

The Life and Legend of an American Pioneer, notes that the "bloodiest and most disastrous [of] British defeats . . . [in] the eighteenth century" was to be the frontiersman's "initiation into forest warfare."

Boone's baptism of blood happened not in Kentucky or Missouri, but on that summer day in 1755. Far from being the ambush depicted by hawkers of broadsheets along Fleet Street in London, or from the printing presses of Beacon Hill in Boston or Southwest Square in Philadelphia, a small garrison of French and Iroquois had actually accidentally stumbled upon Braddock's men. Braddock was to have come with his own Indian troops, but the sachem Shingas had rescinded his initial offer of assistance when the general informed him that, as regards the fertile Ohio country that lay beyond to the west, "No Savage Should Inherit the Land."

Just as Braddock rejected the Indians' aid, he also rejected their strategic thinking about guerilla warfare. Once his Virginians were engaged in open battle with their adversaries, the Scotsman refused to break from the stiff, regimented, aristocratic manner of fighting that defined British military strategy, while the French (as led by Beaujeu, who would die in that battle) were able to flit between the dense grove of trees, their firing muskets "like Leaves in Autumn," as a survivor wrote.

What followed were three hours of slaughter; though Braddock arrived with over three thousand troops and his enemies had a force only a tenth of that, the day would end with close to 500 dead British soldiers and an equivalent number of wounded, while the French suffered only twenty-seven casualties. Boone barely escaped alive, and as he'd poetically recall decades later, "all attempts were in vain, / From sighs and from tears he could scarcely refrain. / Poor Brittons, poor Brittons, poor Brittons remember, / Although we fought hard, we were forced to surrender." According to accounts, the French and their allies alike scalped the fallen British, nailing their pates to the trees that grew upon the bluffs overlooking the tributary.

The Battle of the Monongahela was one of the most spectacular British military losses in the entire Seven Years' War. The bloodshed in North America started a year before the bulk of fighting throughout the globe, triggered at the Battle of Jumonville Glen when a young Virginian colonel and his Indian allies ambushed a contingent of Canadian soldiers, hoping to ultimately begin the dislodging of the French from the Ohio River Valley. Legend recounts that the French commander Joseph Coulon de Jumonville was killed by tomahawk.

Writing in *Crucible of War: The Seven Years' War and the Fate of British North American, 1754–1766,* historian Fred Anderson observes that the violence in western Pennsylvania is the "most important event to occur in eighteenth-century North America," though one which "figures in most Americans' consciousness of the past as a kind of hazy backdrop to the Revolution." Despite its strange invisibility in both our educations and our popular culture, the French and Indian War was responsible not just for the realignment that saw the British dislodge their French adversaries from much of the continent (despite the former's spectacular loss at Monongahela), but which also helped consolidate American identity among a disparate thirteen colonies, set the course of Bourbon foreign policy in the eventual aid of a burgeoning independence movement, and inculcated the economic and political preconditions that made the Revolution itself inevitable. In addition to all of that, Anderson writes that without the war near the woods of Pittsburgh, "it would be difficult to imagine the French Revolution occurring as it did, when it did—or, for that matter, the Wars of Napoleon, Latin America's first independence movements, the transcontinental juggernaut that Americans call 'westward expansion,' and the hegemony of English-derived institutions and the English language north of the Rio Grande."

Before all of that, the defeat reverberated in British fear and embarrassment, as surely as Boone would be haunted for his whole life by the image of scalps nailed to trees. Something about such a decisive and imbecilic loss, tended by Braddock's hubris and incompetence, broke something in the American spirit, and contributed to the rapacious sense that the Ohio Valley was not just a place for traders (as with the French), but a location to be settled, a land to be possessed. What one person calls mythmaking, another calls a ghost story. To be haunted is to be haunted regardless of the origins of that specter, and the repercussions can extend far beyond the few hundred who are initially effected.

Literary theorist Richard Slotkin argues in *Regeneration through Violence: The Mythology of the American Frontier, 1600–1860* that "Through myths the psychology and world view of our cultural ancestors are transmitted to modern descendants, in such away and with such power that our perceptions of contemporary reality and our ability to function in the world are directly, often tragically affected." When the American revolutionaries declared their intent to secede from the British Empire, the latter's blocking of colonial settling in the West (in deference to Indian allies in the Ohio region) was a central plank in American dissatisfaction with the monarch and Parliament. For veterans of that initial trauma, there was a haunting that could only be exorcised with a show of strength, a virile statement of national self-determination, a lust for acquiring that forbidden land beyond the Ohio.

The colonel who'd started the war at Jumonville Glen would be a survivor of Monongahela, and though he'd carry Braddock's sash with him into battle for the rest of his life, he'd write that the British reaction was such that they "struck with such a panic that they behaved with more cowardice than it is possible to conceive." When it came to rectification for such a nosebleed, George Washington wouldn't forget those lessons that were imparted at Monongahela.

Biological Warfare at Fort Pitt

Inside Fort Pitt's timbered walls, it would have always smelled of wood fire. Dirt would have always been beneath the nails of soldiers and civilians; pig grease would have coated their palms. The odor of offal and shit would have hung like miasma around the hazy embankments. It would be impossible not to have some discomfort here, at the very ends of the earth, in this new settlement to be named for the prime minister and pronounced "Pitts-borough" in the proper Scots manner. By 1763, several hundred women, men, and children were crowded into two fortified acres, with additional lodgings extending to the riverbanks. By the spring, those buildings would be abandoned, for May 27 marked the beginning of a brutal, three-month siege as Odawa scouts attempted to dislodge the English. An Irish fur trader named George Croghan observed that "all the Indian nations . . . became very Jealous of the English, who had erected so many Posts in their Country, but were not so generous to them as the French, and particularly gave them no Ammunition, which was the cause of their Jealousy and Discontent."

Named for the chief who was its leader, Pontiac's Rebellion saw several English fortifications in what had once been New France fall, with Fort Pitt's siege preceded by the collapse of Sandusky, Presque Isle, and Detroit. Scholar Gordon M. Sayre, in *The Indian Chief as Tragic Hero: Native Resistance in the Literatures of America, from Montezuma to Tecumseh,* writes that figures like Pontiac "were the tragic heroes of America. The Indian leaders' nobility, ambition, and courage as well as their flaws and their demises were portrayed with all the dignity accorded the greatest characters" of the Western canon. Who should hold dominion over the massive interior of North America was no foregone conclusion; the Treaty of Paris had theoretically ensured British hegemony in the region, but that was meaningless without Indian assistance. Pontiac didn't assent to the supposed new order, especially once the English began to immediately renege on their treaties with the Indians. As Pontiac's ally, the Shawnee Chief Turtleheart told Captain Simeon Ecuyer of Fort Pitt, "You marched your armies into our country, and built forts here, though we told you, again and again, that we wished you to move. This land is ours, and not yours."

With Fort Pitt once again the western terminus of British North America, soldiers and civilians alike hunkered down into the narrow plot of land at the peninsula of the Ohio's forks. That summer, a combined force of Seneca, Delaware, and Mingo Indians unsuccessfully tried to dislodge the settlement, whose geographic placement and fortifications helped it to hold longer than had the other British forts. It's hard not to sympathize with the civilians, though it's much harder to empathize with the architects of colonial policy, as the officers who governed Fort Pitt contrived an evil policy that would decimate the Indians of the Ohio River Valley. Allied and belligerent alike, both soldier and innocent, felled by an ingeniously malignant invention—biological warfare.

Swiss-born Colonel Henry Bouquet would conceive of something heinous, an incontrovertible war crime and an aid to ethnic cleansing and genocide. Bouquet wrote, "Could it not be contrived to send the small pox among the disaffected tribes of Indians? . . . I will try to inoculate the Indians by means of the Blankets that may fall in their hands." Under the guise of presenting peace offerings, the military would distribute objects of infection. Blankets used to swaddle babies and to comfort the ill, to swath the elderly and to cover newlyweds, would disperse smallpox, which had killed millions of Indians over the previous two centuries.

That Pontiac's Rebellion was brutal to settlers is true; often unspeakable violence was committed against colonists. Yet that can be true and it can also be true that Bouquet's evil idea opened a new chapter in the history of human belligerence. When the Puritans arrived on New England's rocky shoals, when Cavaliers came to Jamestown, when Hernán Cortés invaded the Aztecs, and when Francisco Pizzaro conquered the Incas, smallpox acted as what the literary theorist Stephen Greenblatt called "invisible bullets" in advance of the Europeans who would build their homes upon the ruins. But Bouquet was the first to do this deliberately.

Furthermore, it must be remembered that Bouquet actually approved its use against *peaceful* Indians. Militia Commander William Trent noted how Bouquet gave the diseased articles to Turtlehead and other friendly Indians as a (cursed) peace offering. Trent wrote in his diary, "Out of our regard to them we gave them two Blankets and an Handkerchief out of the Small Pox Hospital. I hope it will have the desired effect." That this was done not just in attack against Pontiac, but as an act of extermination against all Indians, is clear in a letter from General Jeffrey Amhert where he writes, "You will do well to try to inoculate the Indians by means of blankets, as well as to try every other method that can serve to extirpate this execrable race."

Robert Harris and Jeremy Paxman, in *A Higher Form of Killing: The Secret History of Chemical and Biological Warfare,* write that "germ weapons turn civilization on its head. Diseases are not fought, but carefully cultivated; doctors use their knowledge of the functions of the human body to devise ever more effective means of halting those functions." Epidemiologists and demographers estimate that as many as a million and a half Indians in the Ohio Territory would die from smallpox over the next few decades—friend and foe alike, warfaring and peaceful alike, soldier and civilian alike, adult and child alike.

The Ill-Fated Vandalia Colony

Pittsburgh was the first metropolis of the Appalachian frontier. So much of American regional identity was shaped by historical events in the subsequent century, but divisions between North and South, East and West, were not intrinsic—born rather from arbitrary distinctions that could shift. Pittsburgh was a relative latecomer in the history of early American colonization. Maybe it would be more accurate to say that Pittsburgh is among the "Oldest New Places," the first of the westward settlements that would eventually stretch to the Pacific. More than a century separates Fort Pitt from Jamestown, New Amsterdam, and Boston—even Philadelphia is almost a hundred years older.

As Fort Pitt transformed into Pittsburgh, her reputation as the gateway to the West was earned in economic importance, and ambiguous geography as well. Such is the uncertainty of the frontier; it rejects the certainty of the border in favor of an ever-shifting and expanding field. Historian Frederick Jackson Turner, in his classic 1893 essay, "The Significance of the Frontier in American History," claimed that this was a country defined by "coarseness and strength combined with acuteness and inquisitiveness," the domain of a "restless, nervous energy; that dominant individualism, working for good and evil . . . [an] exuberance which comes with freedom."

No contemporary American metropolis exists at the confluence of three major geographic regions—technically in the Northeast, often thought of as midwestern, and only a few clicks above the Mason-Dixon Line. "Northeast," "Midwest," and the "South" are all arbitrary constructions, having little to do with hill and mountain, stream and river. What would be more accurate is to understand that Pittsburgh was, and always has been, Appalachian.

In the late eighteenth century, no settlement of English-speakers had a higher population in the Appalachians, and that remains true. Pittsburgh radically differed from Puritan Boston, Dutch Reformed New York, Quaker Philadelphia, and Anglican Jamestown. Those whom initially settled Pittsburgh were from the northern English Midlands, the Scottish Lowlands, and Ulster. Here, the English, Scots, and Scots-Irish found a terrain that in hill and green dale reminded them of those places from which they had come, and they exported with them their low church Presbyterian faith. Calvinist Presbyterianism marked western Pennsylvania as sure as the traditionalist Anglicans of the South, the radical Quakers of the East, or the staid Puritans of the North effected their respective regions. For the inheritors of Penn's utopian vision in Philadelphia, the battle-hardened Scots and Scots-Irish provided a convenient means of fighting the Indians and French, Presbyterianism having no pacifist inclinations in need of sublimation.

Historian David Hackett Fischer, in *Albion's Seed: Four British Folkways in America,* argues that regional identity indelibly marked the English, Scottish, and Irish settlers to their respective areas. Just as New England's character was supposedly shaped by Yankee values of thrift and simplicity, or the South's was affected by the Cavalier ethos of tradition and leisure, so Fischer claims that Scottish Presbyterianism gave the Appalachians—on either side of the Mason-Dixon Line—their own distinct identity. Fischer writes of these immigrants that the "speech of these people was English, but they spoke with a lilting cadence that rang strangely in the ear. Many were desperately poor. But even in their poverty they carried themselves with a fierce and stubborn pride that warned others to treat them with respect."

No doubt that description is one that many contemporary Pittsburghers would be attracted to, even as most of our ancestors aren't from Manchester, Glasgow, or Ulster, but rather Dublin, Frankfurt, Hamburg, Naples, Warsaw, Krakow, Budapest, and Prague (not to mention from Richmond, Charleston, and Montgomery). Despite Fischer's merits, it's important not to overly reduce and essentialize—after all, inhabitants of Boston and Philadelphia probably see themselves as having a fierce and stubborn pride as well. Nevertheless, there is a merit to understanding that Pittsburgh isn't Plymouth.

As concerns its home province, Pittsburgh has always been more *in* Pennsylvania than it has been *of* Pennsylvania. In 1769, surveyors in the Grand Ohio Company proposed a new colony to be named in honor of the German-born British Queen: Vandalia. This new territory was to include almost all of present-day West Virginia, large portions of Kentucky, and western Pennsylvania south of the Ohio River with a capital at Fort Pitt. Less than a decade later, and inspired by the ideals of the Revolution in 1776, the yeoman farmers of Allegheny proposed a new state called Westylvania, a "Sister Colony & the fourteenth Province of the American Confederacy," so that the "Said Country be constituted and declared & acknowledged a separate, distinct, and independent Province & Government."

That Vandalia failed, that it isn't "real," underscores the contingencies of geography. That Westylvania was never recognized should be no impediment to acknowledging its existence.

Modern Chivalry

During the 1771 commencement of Princeton's College of New Jersey, New York-born Huguenot Philip Freneau and the Scottish law student Hugh Henry Brackenridge (who immigrated with his family to the backwaters of central Pennsylvania) stood in front of Nassau Hall to recite their prophetic epic with the grandiose title of *The Rising Glory of America*. Framed by heavy gray doors, and underneath the columned portico and modest dome, the two thundered their declaration, for America was as a "new Jerusalem sent down from heav'n . . . to live and reign on earth a thousand years / Thence call'd Millennium." The wilds of Pennsylvania were "Paradise a new."

Freneau and Brackenridge were members of a radical cohort that began to dream in millennial terms. First poets of a new patriotism, Freneau and Brackenridge fumbled toward an idiom to express their political sentiments on the verge of Revolution. "By freedom blest and richly stor'd with all / The luxuries of life," Freneau would read in his Yankee accent; "Hail happy land / The seat of empire the bode of kings, / The final stage where time shall introduce/Renowned characters and glorious works," responded Brackenridge in a brogue tempered by York, Pennsylvania. Six years later, a cannonball would fly through Nassau Hall's front window at the Battle of Princeton, supposedly obliterating the face on a portrait of King George III. Twelve years after, Nassau Hall would be the temporary capitol of the new United States of America.

The central theme of *The Rising Glory of America* is of transformation, of the ways in which the New World supposedly offers a new dawn to Britain's fading dusk. Brackenridge was transformed in a different way, first moving to Philadelphia but finding the growing city of 30,000 people to be overwhelming. Writing in 1781, Brackenridge remarked of Philadelphia that "I saw no chance for being anything in that city, there were such great men before me." And so, like so many of his fellow Hibernians, Brackenridge sought a different fortune, in that village of 400 people on the western frontier.

When Brackenridge arrived, Pittsburgh was simply a thin strip of dirt paths along the sides of the rivers. In Philadelphia, citizens could read Benjamin Franklin's *Pennsylvania Gazette,* but Pittsburghers had no newspaper, so Brackenridge founded the *Pittsburgh Gazette.* Ever the polymath, Franklin had also established for the people of Philadelphia the University of Pennsylvania; since Pittsburgh was lacking in a similar institution of higher education, Brackenridge would establish the Pittsburgh Academy, known today as the University of Pittsburgh.

Brackenridge was a western Franklin, the jurist, educator, and journalist of this nascent metropolis. He was also the first major writer of the frontier. Among the cobblestoned streets of Philadelphia's Southwest Square, Charles Brockden Brown wrote *Wieland: Or; the Transformation: An American Tale,* and *Edgar Huntley; or, Memoirs of a Sleepwalker,* but on the dirt paths of Pittsburgh, Brackenridge would compose *Modern Chivalry: Containing the Adventures of Captain John Farrago and Teague O'Regan, His Servant,* a sprawling, maximalist, romantic, metafictional picaresque. Published in 1792, six years before Brockden Brown's, the novel is among the first to be published in the United States.

Modern Chivalry's subject is the perambulations of Farrago, who alongside his own Sancho Panza, the drunken Irish layabout O'Regan, envisions a new society stretching along towards the dusk. Brackenridge's editor Ed White writes that "More than any other novel of the period, it takes up the details of political and cultural controversies . . . treating a host of new cultural institutions and political battles." Brackenridge's modernization of the sixteenth-century Spanish novelist Miguel de Cervantes's classic *Don Quixote* has Farrago riding "about the world a little, with his man Teague at his heels, to see how things were going on here and there, and to observe human nature."

If the voice of Farrago sounds a bit like his creator, that's not a mistake. *Modern Chivalry's* theme is invention, and in that space the plot isn't just about Farrago and O'Regan, but about the possibility of moving to the West and making a new name for yourself. In that sense, *Modern Chivalry* is about Brackenridge; it's about America; it's about Pittsburgh. As Brackenridge would reflect on his new home, he had offered "myself to the place" so as "to advance the country and thereby myself."

When Brackenridge arrived, Pittsburgh was more of an idea than a reality. He identified a need, envisioned a solution, and so invented an entire city.

The First Iron Forge

Iron has been smelted, heated, pounded out of various compounds and minerals for five millennia. Extracting iron from its oxidized form requires much greater temperatures than the equivalent metallurgical processes for substances like tin and copper; the development of iron-working thus represents a paradigm shift in technological capability and marked the ascension of the Sumerians and the Hittites, the Egyptians and the Greeks. Anthropologist Jared Diamond writes in *Guns, Germs, and Steel: The Fates of Human Societies* that "iron ore metallurgy grew out of thousands of years of human experience with natural outcrops of pure metals soft enough to be hammered into shape." Artifacts are found in abundance some twelve centuries before the Common Era, in tombs and graveyards, royal storehouses and temples, from China to the Celtic fringe, from Zimbabwe to the North Sea. In the earliest version of the process, iron was extracted through kilns known as bloomeries, ovens capable of reaching a high enough temperature through burning carbon-rich charcoal, air bellowing through the chimneys of the clay structure.

Two years after Brackenridge arrived in Pittsburgh, the British ironmaster Peter Onions developed the "Puddling Process" at his forge in Dowlais, Wales. In the Puddling Process, a kiln is heated from burning coke or coal rather than charcoal. With higher temperatures, more and better iron could be produced more efficiently, and so the blast furnace was introduced as an integral part of the Industrial Revolution, born out of the scientific and engineering enthusiasms of the Enlightenment. British deforestation eliminated easy access to the wood required for charcoal, so it became imperative for the growing iron industry to locate itself near readily available sources of coal.

Despite this, charcoal was the fuel of the Shadyside Iron Furnace, the first forge within Pittsburgh, founded in 1793. Three business associates, German immigrant George Anshutz, Anthony Beelen, and William Amberson alighted for the flat land a few miles east of Pittsburgh and constructed that small plant for processing iron ore, specifically in the production of stoves and grates. The furnace would suffer from its reliance on charcoal, since the settlement didn't have access to major sources of timber, as well as from Pittsburgh's relative distance from sources of iron ore, with the plant closing after just a year.

The failure of the Shadyside Iron Furnace became a footnote, a historical curiosity, with Anshutz's foundery having no discernable role in the development of Pittsburgh's future iron industry. It was but a slight orange glow from the simple foundry in the woods, lighting up the path from the settlement at the forks to points further east. Even though it would be sixty-five years before another iron furnace would operate in Allegheny County, the area would eventually become the preeminent iron manufacturing location on Earth. As American blast furnaces adapted to coal rather than charcoal, Pittsburgh's anthracite-rich location became advantageous. The city rested on a river that was the gateway to the massive western interior, making fully a third of the United States reachable as the Ohio flowed toward the Mississippi. As a way of hypothesizing as to what attracted Anshutz, a Strasbourg-born ironmaster, from Alsace to the hinterlands of the new republic, historian Marcellin C. Adams explained that "even in those early days, people seemed to have a vision of what America might become and realized the strategic position that Pittsburgh occupied in regard to the development of business in the West."

The area that got its name from the furnace would eventually become a prosperous suburb of the city, and then eventually a central neighborhood as Pittsburgh expanded out. In a region known for its industrial communities, from Jonestown and Altoona in Pittsburgh's countryside, to Monongahela and McKeesport in its inner-ring, and the Southside and Lawrenceville within the city itself, the place where Pittsburgh's industrial history originated would ironically never be known for such.

"Interestingly," Quintin R. Skrabec writes in *The World's Richest Neighborhood: How Pittsburgh's East Enders Forged American Industry*, "the furnace was within a mile of the future homes of America's greatest iron, steel, and coke masters of the next century." Rather than foundries, Shadyside had brownstones and townhouses; rather than factories, there were mansions. Anshutz, Beelan, and Amberson built their furnace in Shadyside, but eventually Shadyside would be built by furnaces.

Whiskey Rebels March

In April 1794, former president of the Committee of Public Safety Georges Danton would discover that the French Revolution was cannibalizing itself, and so as one of the thousands of victims of the Reign of Terror, he laid his head beneath the guillotine blade. A month later, the Jacobin radical Maximilien Robespierre, president of the National Convention, officially abolished Catholicism as the faith of France, replacing it with a Cult of the Supreme Being. A month after that, Robespierre's head was severed from his neck.

Around that same time, but thousands of miles across the Atlantic in western Pennsylvania, the "Liberty Poles" of the French Revolution began to be erected upon town squares. In settlements like Bedford and Somerset, Washington and Carlisle, the Liberty Pole became a symbol of resistance, an adaptation of the pagan Maypole framed by the red felt of the Phrygian cap, so as to signify that these were an emancipated people.

Often inscribed with a banner that read "Liberty and No Excise," leaders of the new constitutional republic to the east feared what the poles represented—that the countryside around Pittsburgh was enthralled to Jacobin radicalism. By the summer, the countryside had broken out into open revolt, the so-called "Whiskey Rebellion." It was led in part by a lawyer named David Bradford, who had begun to think of himself as a sort of American Robespierre, just weeks after the Incorruptible's blood had pooled on a Parisian scaffold. No less than President Washington remarked that the rebels were engaged in "diabolical attempts to destroy the best fabric of human government and happiness that has ever been presented for the acceptance of mankind," a heady appraisal of a revolt that began in response to an alcohol tax.

Much of how the Whiskey Rebellion is remembered is due to an act of marketing framed by its opponents, the name coined by Secretary of the Treasury Alexander Hamilton. He understood that memorializing the insurrection as the action of drunken country bumpkins obscured the legitimate grievances of the movement. What the Whiskey Rebellion actually represented, if in part a strange echo of Jacobinism in Pittsburgh, was the first concentrated opposition to the new constitutional order that had eliminated the anarchic and democratic potential of the Articles of Confederation. Contemporary eastern accounts of the uprising condemned this "total subversion of government"; Federalists and anti-Jeffersonians besmirched the rebels as "vipers who would overturn all order, government, and laws."

Historian Thomas R. Slaughter writes in *The Whiskey Rebellion: Frontier Epilogue to the American Revolution* that for rebels, and sometimes fellow travelers, moderates, and radicals alike, including Bradford, Brackenridge, Albert Gallatin, William Findley, and the mystical-minded hermit, Herman Husband, the insurrection took the "French Revolution as their context and seminal cause for the Rebellions." According to Slaughter, such "Jacobin ideals had come to infect the 'sans culottes of Pittsburgh.'" He records that there was rumor in the East that the rebels intended to fully secede from the United States, and in the process rename Washington County as "La Vendee" and Pittsburgh as "Lyons." For many of the rebels, Pittsburgh was also called "Sodom," a symbol of cosmopolitan decadence that stoked the evangelical minds of farmers on the cusp of what would be the Second Great Awakening. A more sensible marriage than might first be surmised, this was a union of secular utopianism and religious millennialism, for both sides saw the Whiskey Rebellion as an opportunity to once again remake the world anew.

As a conflagration, the Rebellion saw more than 7,000 volunteers march on Pittsburgh, the capturing of armories, the death and arrest of conspirators, and the rise of an army of over 12,000 Virginians, Philadelphians, Marylanders, and New Jerseyans personally led by President George Washington. By all credible and fair accounting, it's more accurate to regard the Whiskey Rebellion as an aborted revolution, or as America's first civil war (even while its final death toll was just a handful of people). Despite being treated as a footnote, the Whiskey Rebellion would see torched farms, the tarring and feathering of tax collectors, the destruction of the wealthy Brigadier General John Neville's homestead, the arrest and trial of twenty men brought back in chains to Philadelphia, and Bradford's exile. When an assembled militia gathered at the site of Braddock's defeat to march on Pittsburgh, the expected toll of violence didn't quite reach the crescendo feared by authorities, but the property targeted was entirely that of the rich. The class politics of the Whiskey Rebellion couldn't have been clearer.

Separatist fervor, in part, was born from the distrust between East and West, which had only hardened after the end of the American Revolution. The political issues of the rebellion, however, were more complicated. Since 1791, discontent was brewing over the first levying of a federal tax on a domestic product, and while the Whiskey Rebellion can be misremembered as some sort of libertarian revolt against big government, the reality was actually the opposite. Whiskey was a convenient way for small frontier farms to preserve their grain, and in the West it sometimes functioned as a veritable currency. Hamilton's tax was profoundly regressive, tipped in its balance to favor big business in the East. (You'll note that one of the largest distilleries in the United States was at Washington's Mt. Vernon plantation.) The levy has been interpreted by historians as marking the ascendance of the corporate state.

William Hogeland writes in *The Whiskey Rebellion: George Washington, Alexander Hamilton, and the Frontier Rebels Who Challenged America's Newfound Sovereignty* that the conflict was a "primal national drama that pitted President Washington and other eastern founders, along with their well-heeled frontier proteges and allies . . . against western laborers with a radical vision of the American future." Such was a Manichean struggle of business against the people, but there was no revolution that would happen in Pittsburgh. One of the victims would be that old radical Husband, the mystical prophet of Pittsburgh's woods who dreamt of a utopian New Jerusalem that would descend onto the Alleghenies. He was hauled off to Philadelphia to be tried for treason but was acquitted in part due to his infirmities. On his way back over the mountains, he caught chill and died.

Sganyadái:yo

One day in 1798, the Indian sachem Sganyadái:yo, who was on a trade mission from upstate New York, hit what recovering alcoholics call their "rock bottom" while in Pittsburgh. Better known by his English name, Handsome Lake, the sachem was half-brother to a Seneca chief named Cornplanter and was tasked to lead a group of hunters through the verdant Allegheny Mountains to trade buckskin and venison in exchange for needed supplies in the village of Jenuchshadego. The Iroquois Confederation had suffered in the second half of the eighteenth century; disease had run rampant through their traditional strongholds of western Pennsylvania and upstate New York, and they were forced into increasingly small reservations by the new republic. Cornplanter had allied his band of Seneca with the British during the Revolutionary War, and the Americans had punished the Indians with increasingly unfair treaties. After the smallpox pandemic, both poverty and alcoholism had reduced the population even further. Religious studies scholar Peter Manseau writes in *One Nation, Under Gods: A New American History* that the Seneca had "begun to poison themselves with the spirits they had learned to drink from those who took their land," as indeed Handsome Lake had been doing for many years.

When the sachem arrived in Pittsburgh, he and his mission traded all that they had hunted and gathered, all that had been cleaned and treated, all that had been sewn and stitched, in exchange for a barrel of the whiskey that the rebels had been fighting to leave untaxed. A strange poetry to a Quaker rhyme Handsome Lake would have perhaps learned from missionaries: "My son, do no ill. / Go not in the way of bad men. / For bad men go to the pit." There is something prophetic to that warning, and more appropriate in its language than the compilers could have known. Handsome Lake drank his whiskey at a location within the confines of the small settlement of Pittsburgh, west of Grant Street and along the banks of the Allegheny, not far from where Meriwether Lewis and William Clark's keelboat would be built and sailed in only four years later.

Manseau records that "For the return trip home, the hunters had lashed their canoes together into a single barge and managed to make their way upriver as the liquor continued to flow. The most inebriated stayed in the center of the flotilla, while those less likely to topple overboard manned the paddles on either side." By the time the drunken party arrived back in Jenuchshadego, they had been reduced to a bestial state. A contemporary account records that upon disembarking, the men did "yell and sing like demented people . . . and run about without clothing and all have weapons to injure those whom they meet. Now there are no doors left in the houses for they have all been kicked off." Cornplanter sequestered his brother, who began to suffer the telltale signs of withdrawal and delirium tremens. Meanwhile, he took counsel with a group of Philadelphia Quakers whom he'd allowed to evangelize amongst the Seneca, who advised that Handsome Lake be treated with charity during his convalescence—his daughter remembered him as being nothing but "yellow skin and dried bones." Manseau notes how Handsome Lake had recounted that as he suffered, "he meditated on the rising and setting of the sun, the stars he could see when staring up through the chimney beside his bed, and the birds he could hear singing in the morning." And then, one day, after the night terrors and fever had subsided, Handsome Lake called his brother and family into the longhouse he had been in.

"Never have I seen such wondrous visions!" the sachem declared, and from that initial recounting of Handsome Lake's visitation by three angelic intermediaries would be born a new faith known as Gaihwi:io—the "Good Message." Handsome Lake would amend the teachings of Deganawida, becoming prophet to a new revelation called the Code of Handsome Lake, and the founder of the Longhouse Religion, a faith that transformed Seneca communities of the early nineteenth century. Handsome Lake's syncretic genius was such that he was able to hybridize the Christian narrative he learned from the Quakers with indigenous belief, so as to form something completely new. The sachem's religion was no mere Christianity in disguise. He was not secretly evangelizing for the faith of his people's oppressors, but as Manseau argues, the Longhouse Religion was "a rebuke, in religious terms, of the entire European endeavor in America."

The Longhouse Religion is arguably many things—a successful syncretic faith, an anti-colonial theology of liberation, and the first widespread movement that centered on recovery from alcoholism. Instrumental to the Code of Handsome Lake was the sachem's revelation concerning how Satan enticed Columbus into "discovering" America. Handsome Lake preached that the Great Deceiver had told Columbus that "[a]cross the ocean that lies toward the sunset is another world and a great country and a people whom you have never seen. . . . Those people are virtuous, they have no unnatural evil habits and they are honest. A great reward is yours if you will help me." To facilitate the fall of this Edenic paradise, Satan gifted Columbus "a flask of rum, a pack of playing cards, a handful of coins, a violin and a decayed leg bone." From those cursed objects, the Europeans encouraged idleness, greed, illness, and drunkenness.

Manseau writes that the prophet had "wondered if whisky was the cause not only of his own illness but of the straits in which his people now found themselves." The result was that following Handsome Lake's beginnings, the United States would birth everything from the Washingtonian Temperance Society of the nineteenth century to Alcoholics Anonymous of today. Writing in *Drunks: An American History*, Christopher M. Finan notes that Handsome Lake was a prophet who while "on the verge of death experienced a vision that caused him to stop drinking," and that he was also "the leader of a religious revival that significantly reduced alcoholism." Indeed, Finan holds that since it was central to Handsome Lake's prophecy that liquor was a narcotic whose specific purpose was the anesthetizing of humans, his code should be seen as the first recovery movement in American history.

A few months after Handsome Lake's revelation, the fires of revival would begin to burn along the Allegheny ridge of his native New York, down through Pennsylvania and into the southern Appalachians. He heralded, in many ways, the beginning of a period of religious genius that's arguably one of the most fertile in American history. Writing in *The American Religion*, literary critic Harold Bloom claimed that our national religion is a type of Gnosticism built on self-reliance and individuality. He writes that "Salvation, for the American, cannot come through the community or the congregation, but is a one-on-one act of confrontation." A wrestling with God and our demons, our vices and our holiness. In Handsome Lake's Code, an immaculate religion was born, for salvation can only come after the fall, or for a barrel of proffered whiskey purchased in Pittsburgh.

PART II

CITY OF BRICK AND TIRED WOOD

Industry, Labor, and Growth

(1800–1899)

Harmony

Long before the flames of revival metaphorically scorched the Earth in what's known as the "Burned-Over District," the mountainous thread from upstate New York into Kentucky, Pennsylvania had been a haven for religious dissenters looking for freedom of conscience. During the colonial era, the Quaker province had been only the third place on Earth to offer complete religious freedom (after Rhode Island, and for a brief period in the sixteenth century, Transylvania). True to that history, Pennsylvania attracted Anabaptists, Amish, Mennonites, and Moravians. More exotic groups would arrive as well; the apocalyptic-minded Society of the Woman in the Wilderness would settle in Germantown, near Philadelphia, where they'd practice occultism and alchemy while living in hermitages constructed out of caves. Experiments in communal living, such as Ephrata in eastern Pennsylvania, attempted to build a bit of heaven on Earth. As such, this tradition of religious liberty combined with the new enthusiasms of the Second Great Awakening and made the countryside north of Pittsburgh ideal for the establishment of the German Pietist George Rapp's utopia that was to be known as Harmony. "I am a prophet," Rapp had thundered to a German congregation in 1791, "and I am to be known as the one."

Coming to America in 1804 from the Duchy of Württemberg, Rapp was influenced by the theurgy and hermeticism of thinkers like the seventeenth-century German mystic Jacob Böhme and the eighteenth-century Swedish scientist Emanuel Swedenborg, advocating communal property and celibacy. The Harmonists had tremendous economic success, operating a distillery, a sawmill, tanneries, and a vineyard, while making themselves instrumental in the construction of the Pittsburgh and Lake Erie Railroad that would link East and West in the rapidly industrializing nation. Harmony was to be what's known as an "intentional community," a society dedicated to propositions that all members ascent to, with the aim of creating as close to a perfect society as is possible in our profane world. The new community was built around Rapp's 1798 Lomersheimer Declaration, which had abolished baptism and confirmation, relegated communion and confession to annual events, and embraced pacifism and the spurning of state-run schools. As a result, the Harmonists had been greatly persecuted by the Lutheran Church in Germany. They also refused to declare any allegiance to the state, with Rapp writing that "according to the Gospel no oath is allowed him who gives evidence of a righteous life as an upright man."

Disestablishment as promised by the First Amendment, arguably the only unique aspect of American democracy, granted Rapp's Harmonists the opportunity to flourish—which they did. Writing in *Paradise Now: The Story of American Utopianism,* Chris Jennings records that Rapp had "decided that North America, beyond the reach of the corrupt churches of Europe and the Lutheran establishment that had imprisoned him, was that prophesized wilderness—a vast green antechamber to the reign of heaven on earth." Despite a decade-long sojourn in the Indiana wilderness, the Harmonists would make Butler County their home, first in Harmony and then in a town called Economy, with the community growing to a thousand individuals. From their factories eighteen miles north of Pittsburgh, the Harmonists would produce wooden furniture, wine, beer, and even silk, dominating several markets of home goods. Jennings writes that the Harmonists, and those in their stead, "intended to catalyze a global revolution by building a working prototype of the ideal society."

There was something prototypically American about these strange Germans, the utopian yearning enacted through crassly capitalist means, holiness and hokum in equal measure. Stephen Prothero writes in *American Jesus: How the Son of God Became a National Icon* that the country is a "sprawling spiritual marketplace, where religious shoppers can choose among all the world's great religions," just as surely as how, in the first decades of the nineteenth century, a Pittsburgher could buy a bottle of wine or a bolt of silk from a Harmonist plying his wares in Market Square. For a brief period, Pittsburgh was a buckle on the belt of the Second Great Awakening, Husband's dream for a New Jerusalem where new gods were being born again.

In 1812, two years before Rapp would abscond with the Harmonists to Indiana (only to return in the following decade), a Revolutionary War veteran and Congregationalist minister named Solomon Spalding, who'd moved to Pittsburgh from his native Connecticut, was busy accidentally creating his own new religion. It was in Pittsburgh where Spalding finished his unpublished historical romance, *Manuscript, Found*. Telling an imagined story about how the pre-Columbian Indian burial mounds that dot the Appalachians had been constructed by seafaring Romans, *Manuscript, Found* bore some similarity to the revelations received by another upstate New York prophet named Joseph Smith.

The book was shelved indefinitely, and then lost by the Pittsburgh publishers of Patterson & Lambdin, who did not have the financial resources to fund *Manuscript, Found*. Spalding's brother would swear in an affidavit that he remembered that the novel took as its subject "that the American Indians are the descendants of the Jews . . . [an] account of their journey from Jerusalem . . . until they arrived in America, under the command of Nephi and Lehi. . . . Cruel and bloody wars ensued, in which great multitudes were slain. They buried their dead in large heaps, which caused the mounds so common in this country."

Ironically, no original version of *Manuscript, Found* exists, making it difficult to ascertain the plagiarism accusations against Smith's *Book of Mormon*. The affidavit is often quoted in anti-Latter Day Saints polemics, but it's hard to see how Smith could have discovered this unpublished manuscript that was finished when he was only seven. True to the stipulations of the Second Great Awakening, such issues must forever be deferred to faith.

"Beautiful Dreamer"

On July 4, 1826, John Adams died in Quincy, Massachusetts. On the same day, hundreds of miles south, Thomas Jefferson died at his plantation in Charlottesville, Virginia. In between, at the western frontier town of Pittsburgh, a baby named Stephen Foster was born who, though white, would grow up harboring the ambition to become the "best Ethiopian songwriter."

Jefferson and Adams, even with all of their ideological divergences, embodied a dry Enlightenment understanding of what the nation was to be, but Foster's era was not one metaphorically presided over by Jefferson's arid trinity of Bacon, Locke, and Newton, but rather by a mixture of capitalism, carnival, crackpot religion, hucksterism, medicine show, and tent revival. Foster was to be the one who drafted the soundtrack for that new America, a nation described by critic Greil Marcus as "that old, weird America."

This was a land that had begun to thrill to the culture of the very people that the nation had enslaved. Historian Eric Lott succinctly described this cultural process as "love and theft" in his study of the same name. Foster's nation was one in which more than 1.5 million people—more than 15 percent of the population—were held in bondage. By the census year following the composer's birth, the number of slaves would surpass two million, a reality that de Tocqueville described as defining a nation "covered with a layer of democratic paint," but where the full depth of inequity and injustice couldn't help but be visible. This was the context for the composition of Foster's melodies. He was the first American to earn his fortune entirely from his songs, including through performances and sale of sheet music, even though he would ultimately lose it all.

Editors of the *Penguin Dictionary of American Folklore* duly inform us that Foster's music was incredibly popular in the decades around the Civil War, yet today his tunes are so universal that Foster's work is "often branded indiscriminately as 'traditional music.'" Songs such as "Oh! Susanna!," "Camptown Races," "My Old Kentucky Home," and "Beautiful Dreamer" may not recommend themselves to many as much more than hokey remnants of the nineteenth century, but they remain firmly entrenched in the American canon despite their often racially problematic content. Defenders have argued that Foster's music subtly encoded an abolitionist politics, yet when it came to the true price of the cruelties of slavery, his songs are mute. Foster preferred rather to adopt the persona of the "Beautiful dreamer," where "Starlight and dewdrops are waiting for thee; / Sounds of the rude world heard in the day, / Lull'd by the moonlight have all pass'd away."

Though born in a Northern free state, where politics often veered toward the abolitionist on account of the radical Quaker tradition, Foster is commonly misremembered as the bard of Southern plantation life, of fields "where the sugar-canes grow," of a narrator who comes "from Alabama /With my banjo on my knee," and who in mimicry of Black vernacular is "Still longing for de old plantation, / And for de old folks at home." Yet his Southern-style lyrics were written in the haze of an almost prototypical Northern industrial city. Foster only ventured south of the Ohio River once in his life. Novelist Steve Erickson, in an essay about Foster, claims that his song's "exquisite perversity . . . is that they're steeped not in the American South [but] in a vision of it." Foster's introduction to the South came at the tutelage of his family's biracial servant, Olivia Pise, whom he accompanied as a child to a Black church service in Pittsburgh, the first time he had ever heard the music he'd spend a career imitating. According to Erickson, it's these "wafts of magnolia, the unresolved American contradictions" that "rage in Foster's music." Foster doesn't offer us verisimilitude, but rather perfumed dreams. A cynic might claim that the fantasies of Foster, with his obscuring of the barbarism, savagery, and violence that made the material comforts of that society possible, are not just a darkly occluded dream, but rather a version of the American Dream.

Not coincidentally, and only a few years after Foster was born, a performer from New York's Lower East Side named Thomas Dartmouth "Daddy" Rice invented one of the most disturbingly enduring of American archetypes, based on a cruel pantomime of a crippled, Black stable hand, who in some accounts Rice met while on tour in Pittsburgh, and who would come to be known as "Jim Crow." Rice and Foster were first of a type it would seem; in *Hip: The History,* music critic John Leland identifies them as the germinating seeds in a family tree that would include "Irving Berlin, Al Jolson, Mezz Mezzrow, Carl Van Vechten, Elvis and Eminem . . . the white boys who stole the blues." An 1867 eulogy for Foster from the *Atlantic Monthly,* written three years after Foster squandered his royalties and died drunk in Manhattan's Bellevue Hospital with only thirty-eight cents cents in his pocket, includes one account of such a theft of the blues at Rice's first Jim Crow show, in Pittsburgh. The author soberly records the "entertainment" to be had at the expense of a Black bellhop named Cuff who worked at the Griffith Hotel on Wood Street, "an exquisite specimen of his sort." The author writes that "Rice, having shaded his own countenance to the 'contraband' hue, ordered Cuff to disrobe, and proceeded to invest himself in the cast-off apparel . . . the extraordinary apparition produced an instant effect. . . . The effect was electric."

And so, the effect has remained electric, as white performers from Rice to Miley Cyrus have stolen the proverbial "cast-off

AN ALTERNATIVE HISTORY OF PITTSBURGH

apparel" of Black artists. There's "love and theft" again, though one would be forgiven for focusing more on the theft than the love. Scholar W. T. Lhamon Jr. explains that the minstrel show, with its combination of grossly stereotypical music, dance, and humor, "provided talismans of Blackness that people with more power could warp to their prejudices. And they did." The grotesque, broad red smile and pearly teeth of the corked blackface "Jim Crow" character haunts American popular culture, and in the nineteenth century, the ballads and jigs that he shuffled to were often written by the songwriter born in Lawrenceville, Pennsylvania. There is an obscenity to the whole of the thing: white performers filching Black melodies, used to mock those very same Black lives from which those songs originated.

Free Soil

Martin Delany first came to Pittsburgh at the age of nineteen. Before that, he'd lived in Chambersburg, just a scant thirteen miles north of the Mason-Dixon line and the slavery in which all of his extended family were held. Before Pennsylvania, he'd been raised in Charles Town, Virginia (now West Virginia). His maternal grandparents were Mandinka, of the Niger Valley, and his father's people came from the Gola of Liberia. In America, only his mother was free, though by Virginia's antebellum slavery codes, manumission was transmitted through matrilineal descent, and so on either side of the border, Delany was rendered a free man of color. To ensure her son's freedom, Delany's mother had argued his case (and won) in front of a Winchester, Virginia, courthouse; the move to Pennsylvania was to guarantee their state of continued emancipation upon free soil.

By the time Delany absconded to Pittsburgh, the city was a growing metropolis. Paved roads and redbrick sidewalks defined the streets in a growing downtown, the hazy miasma of chimney smoke and industry hanging in the air. Delany would settle in a neighborhood taking shape on an eastern ridge overlooking the central business district that came to be known as the Hill District, which remains a center of Black life in Pittsburgh today. There, Delany would apprentice with a white physician, become the first enrolled Black man at the Harvard Medical School (even as the students in supposedly progressive Boston successfully voted to rescind his acceptance), set up practice as Pittsburgh's only Black doctor, and be one of only a few who would work through the deadly cholera epidemics of 1833 and 1854. Delany would also open up a print shop in the environs of the Trinity AME Church on Wylie Avenue, where he'd produce a newspaper with the evocative name of the *Mystery,* whose central political rallying cry would be "Africa for Africans," as the doctor become the first proponent for Black nationalism in the United States.

Delaney's the *Mystery* charted a course far more radical than even abolitionist newspapers like William Lloyd Garrison's the *Liberator* or Frederick Douglass's the *North Star.* Whenever speaking engagements brought Garrison and Douglass through Pittsburgh, they'd make calls on Delany at his Hill District practice. It was only the *Mystery*, though, that advocated for the establishment of a "Black Israel" on the West African coast. Robert S. Levine writes in *Martin Delany, Frederick Douglass, and the Politics of Representative Identity* that "Delany's insistence on his status as a representative and exemplary 'black' man has led to his virtual reification as the Father of Black Nationalism—a radical separatist who ultimately sought to lead blacks back to their 'native' Africa." Levine argues that Delany has been set up in opposition to the seemingly more moderate Douglass (with whom Delany coedited the *North Star* for eighteen months), but that any analysis that reduces the writer's politics "dissolves any simple attempts to fix him as consistently either conservative or radical."

Reacting both to the perfidious arguments of the Southern pro-slavery contingent, as well as the often condescending rhetoric of abolitionists, Delany's politics anticipated Marcus Garvey and Malcolm X. Writing in his 1852 treatise *The Condition, Elevation, Emigration, and Destiny of the Colored People of the United States,* Delany argued that "Politicians, religionists, colonizationists, and abolitionists, have each and all, at different times, presumed to think for, dictate to, and know better what suited colored people, than they knew for themselves." By contrast, Delany was offering a full-throated, proud, vigorous, and unrepentant declaration of Black self-determination. Levine emphasizes that though Delany has often been conflated with separatism, his political thought was complicated and ever evolving. At times, he so despaired at the treatment of Black Americans that he thought only the establishment of a homeland would ensure liberty; at other points, he wrote with enthusiasm for American democracy, going so far as to ultimately become the highest ranking Black officer during the Civil War, present at the rising of the flag above Fort Sumter at the conclusion of the conflict. Writing in an 1845 editorial for the *Mystery,* Delany promised that the "paper shall be free, independent and untrammeled and whilst it shall aim at the Moral Elevation of the Africo American and African race, civilly, politically and religiously, yet, it shall support no distinctive principles of race . . . since whatever is essentially necessary for the promotion and elevation of all classes; therefore our interests are, and should be, one and inseparable."

Delany's political philosophy is perhaps best understood as emphasizing dignity and self-determination as much as anything. Rhetorician and Africana Studies scholar Molefi Kete Asante said at a 2012 Temple University address that Delany was "simply creating a philosophy of recovery, [and] reconstruction of a badly treated people," that he should be seen as a "transformatist" who refused to "accept servility, subservience, and inferiority, but is one who contends that self-identity and the acceptance of self-determination as a motivator of human maturity." Even more than in Delany's explicitly political writings, this is seen in his unheralded masterpiece, the novel *Blake: Or, the Huts of America, A Story of the Mississippi Valley, the Southern United States, and Cuba,* an epic that imagined a massive slave revolt a year before the outbreak of the Civil War. Penned in response to the servile depiction of enslaved people presented in Harriet Beecher Stowe's *Uncle Tom's Cabin,* Delany enshrined "the names of Nat Turner, Denmark Vesey, and General Gabriel." Reflecting on those past rebels, the titular character remarks that these are "the kind of fighting men they then needed among the blacks."

Martha Schoolman explains in her study, *Abolitionist Geographies,* that Delany's novel "marks the fullest expression of literary abolitionism," with his "image of escaping slaves not simply as refugees in need of guidance but as persons technically as well as physically capable of self-liberation." Delany repurposed the melody and lyrics of Foster to entirely different ends, a rhetoric that involves a "complex reinvention of the minstrel tradition" as Lott writes in *Love and Theft,* the novel having made "guerilla appropriations of Stephen Foster plantation melodies, giving them new and often parodic lyrics, and [in] this way furnishes his revels with songs of revolution." Here's Blake, with very different lyrics to the melody of Foster's song: "Hand up the shovel and the hoe-o-o-o! / I don't care whether I work or no! / Old master's gone to the slaveholder's rest— / He's gone where they all ought to go!"

Such was the forbearance of a man who in 1860 would be invited by Lord Henry Brougham, First Baron Brougham and Vaux, to address the International Statistical Society at London's Somerset House so as to answer questions regarding his successful treatment of the 1854 Pittsburgh cholera outbreak. In attendance was President James Buchanan's Ambassador to the Court of St. James, George Mifflin Dallas, as well as the head of the American delegation to the conference, Augustus Baldwin Longstreet. Both men were committed slavers, representing the Pennsylvania-born president's policy of appeasement to the future Confederacy. Introduced by Brougham, who was a steadfast supporter of emancipation, Delany ascended the dais, looked toward Dallas and Longstreet, and said, "I rise, your Royal Highness, to thank his Lordship, the unflinching friend of the Negro, for the remarks he has made to myself and to assure your Royal Highness and his Lordship that I am a man." Douglass would reflect that "Sermons in stone are nothing to this."

Delany's act was of the moment. A few months later, a new president would be in the White House, and the nation would be at war with itself.

The Great Fire

The spring of 1845 was unseasonably dry in the rainy city of Pittsburgh. Now a burgeoning metropolis of 20,000 souls packed in at the forks of the Ohio, Pittsburgh sat across the river from the city of Allegheny to the north and the village of Birmingham on the other side of the Monongahela, both to be annexed later in the century. Haze of industry defused in the air, as the riverboat business that had helped to grow Pittsburgh in the first half of the nineteenth century gave way to the fires of iron processing. When the British novelist Charles Dickens made his tour of the United States three years earlier, he noted that the valley formed at the confluence already had a "great quantity of smoke hanging over it," the industrial reputation of Pittsburgh in embryonic form. Another traveler, less famous than the author of *Great Expectations,* records an approach into the city whereby "Pittsburgh was hidden from our view, until we descended through the hills within half a mile of the Allegheny river. Dark dense smoke was rising from many parts, and a hovering cloud of this vapor, obscuring the prospect, rendered it singularly gloomy." Such was the weather in Mulciber's western workshop, posed in language as if taken from Dante and Milton.

The atmosphere was polluted with the coal soot and grit of harder industries, but in that dry April, a heavy dusting of cotton and flour particulate from both textile factories and grain mills hung in the air as well. When an Irish domestic washerwoman named Ann Brooks left a stoked fire intended for her wash unattended, a spark amid this combustible dryness ignited a nearby wooden building, leading to the inferno that would completely level the new city. Just like Mrs. O'Leary and her cow in Chicago three decades later, these events are often pinned on women and immigrants, the better to blame a single individual rather than the environment that lets such conflagrations become possible.

Just as every great city has its university and its newspaper, so every great city must have its formative fire. A baptism of fire seems to be a necessary precondition for any city of world historical consequence, and as London had its apocalyptic burning of 1666 and Chicago its coming fire of 1871, so Pittsburgh too had to be immolated only to rise from the ashes, a wooden phoenix transformed into one of brick and iron. In fire there is a narrative of rebirth; there is, as Pittsburgh would demonstrate, the possibility of erasure and rebuilding. The possibility of starting over, of redefinition.

"The great fire is so overwhelming to those who witness it," writes historian Peter Charles Hoffer in *Seven Fires: The Urban Infernos that Reshaped America,* that "it seems isolated in time and space, without precedent or explanation." Some of this is because of the archetypal connotations of fire, the ways in which its significance seems almost universal across cultures and religions; some of it is also because fire is very hot, very fast, and will very much kill you. Hoffer's contention is born out of eyewitness accounts of the Great Fire of Pittsburgh, with J. Heron Foster writing in *A Full Account of the Great Fire at Pittsburgh, on the Tenth Day of April, 1845* that it is "impossible for anyone, although a spectator of that dreadful scene of destruction . . . to give more than a faint idea of the terrible, the overwhelming calamity which then befell our city, destroying in a few hours the labor of many years, and blasting suddenly the cherished hopes of hundreds—we may say thousands—of our citizens."

Hoffer explains how the fire spread in the easily flammable city, encouraged by the dry conditions and the atmospheric pollution, and by disorganized and competing privatized fire companies. Starting at dawn (whether the fault of Ms. Brooks or any number of other thousands of people who may have let their guard down for a second), the fire quickly spread. "A wall of flame driven by the wind roared down Fourth, Third, Second, Front, and Water streets," writes Hoffer. Quoting an eyewitness, Hoffer writes how the "loftiest buildings had . . . [melted] before the ocean of flame." By riverboat, women and men escaped to Allegheny and Birmingham as the fire raced through the streets unimpeded, without relief. In a place that would come to be punctuated with more bridges than any other city on Earth, Pittsburgh's only bridge at the time would be a casualty of the fire. Delany, from the Hill District, recorded that the fire was "as though impelled by a destroying angel. . . . Never did any event appear more like Judgement day."

Regardless of the cause, either immediate or structural, the Great Fire of Pittsburgh would see a third of the growing city destroyed, a total of 1,200 buildings with a loss of almost $300 million dollars when adjusted for inflation, and the displacement of over half the city's population, even as authorities claimed that only two people would lose their lives. (A dubious assertion.) By the end of the summer, over 500 structures had already been rebuilt, due to a massive domestic and international fundraising campaign, and a testament not just to the fortitude of the populace but to the rising property prices in the desirable "Gateway to the West." Foster writes with civic pride, only months after the fire, that "traces of our disaster are now disappearing before the magic wand of industry and enterprise."

For those who lived through it, the Great Fire of Pittsburgh was an *annus mirabilis,* a hinge in time that marked that which was before and after. "None witnessed the conflagration but know the difficulty of adequately describing it," writes Foster, imploring charity for those trying to describe the "most destructive conflagration it has ever been our lot to describe."

Now, virtually no evidence of the fire, or of the previous city which it transformed, remains. The event has all but been forgotten in Pittsburgh's memory. An apt metaphor for industry and capitalism itself, the rapaciousness of change which transforms like a fire, the burning away of all tradition, history, and traces of the past, whether good or bad. Hoffer writes that the "founders of Pittsburgh welcomed it. Fire and smoke framed their new city in a grimy halo of industriousness." Literally true when considering the economic base of the rapidly expanding iron city, but fire was also a symbol for that which burns through the underbrush and recreates the land again and again—whether it should be or not.

A Scottish Immigrant Comes to Allegheny

The specters of radical change were made manifest in the spring of 1848 in France, Austria, the German states, and what would become Italy. Fundamentally liberal in nature, the revolutions of 1848 were an inchoate assemblage of events, born from profound dissatisfaction at the political, economic, and cultural disparities that defined the old monarchies of Europe. Historian Mike Rapport writes in *1848: Year of Revolutions* that the "political restrictions imposed on Europe could not help but provoke opposition," and so a vanguard fought for the radical principles embodied in the French Revolution six decades before.

The revolutions had begun sprouting from the twin soil of growing national self-determination and philosophical Romanticism. Disparate people with varied aims, most of the revolutionaries were at least united in an embrace of representative democracy and the establishment of freedom of speech and religion. The more extreme agitated for the abolition of private property itself. From the tumult and excitement of the Springtime of the Peoples would arise new leaders: Giuseppe Mazzini in Italy, Pierre-Joseph Proudhon in France, Friedrich Hecker in what would later be Germany. Karl Marx and Friedrich Engels would enthuse in *The Manifesto of the Communist Party,* released that year, that the "proletarians have nothing to lose but their chains. They have a world to win."

In that year of revolutions, one of those proletarians was a thirteen-year-old weaver's son, who with his family left their one-room home in Dunfermline, Scotland, for the promise of

Allegheny City. In keeping with the working-class radicalism of his father, the young Scotsman had been inculcated in the socialist politics of 1848, but by the time the family arrived in Pennsylvania, the promise of those European revolutions was already waning. "We have been beaten and humiliated," Proudhon wrote of the movements' failure, "scattered, imprisoned, disarmed and gagged." Marx wrote that the working class had a world to win, and for the Scottish immigrant named Andrew Carnegie, that prediction at least proved individually true.

There's no extricating Carnegie, the adopted Pittsburgher who would become the richest man who ever lived, from the context of the revolutionary Europe he emigrated from. In Carnegie's Great Britain, emancipatory politics took the form of Chartism, a working-class movement advocating for (among other things) voting rights and labor union organization. Biographer David Nasaw writes in *Andrew Carnegie* that the Scotsman had long "made a great deal of his Chartist ancestors in his *Autobiography* and in later writings and speeches." Yet as Nasaw makes clear, despite the young immigrant's study of socialist books in the libraries of Allegheny City (an affection for lending libraries being one sentiment of public good that never left him), the crossing of the Atlantic had "effectively severed his ties with them and their movement."

Carnegie would become the rarest of creatures—the actually self-made man. In a nation that has produced scores of hagiographies of capitalists, which venerates the myth of the rugged individualist bootstrapper, there have been precious few who actually went from nothing to everything. In no small part due to his own talents, including cunning and guile, the son of a Scottish weaver could become Andrew Carnegie, the American Midas. Central to that transformation, however, was Carnegie's own class betrayals, the tempering and extinction of his radical birthright of which he so long bragged. Nasaw explains that by the time Carnegie was a working man, he may have been "very much a Chartist and a radical in Scottish affairs," but he was "every bit the company man in Pittsburgh."

His wealth was first made in railroads and then by importing the Bessemer mechanism of steel production to his mills that would soon line the riverbanks of the Allegheny and Monongahela Valleys. Ruthlessness and canniness were integral to Carnegie's business genius, even as his later philanthropic ventures (extensive as they were) served to soften his image. A concern for the working class guiltily weighed on his conscience; Carnegie single-handedly made the free public library an instrument of American democracy, even while he steadfastly resisted labor organization among his workers. With a self-serving eye, he could write in his pithily titled 1889 treatise, *The Gospel of Wealth,* that the "problem of our age is the proper administration of wealth, so that the ties of brotherhood may still bind together the rich and poor in harmonious relationship." He borrowed the rhetoric of the 1848 radicals, but the intent couldn't be more conservative. Wealth isn't to be administered by those who make it, or by the elected democracies representing the popular will of the people. Wealth was to be administered by those who knew best. Specifically, by Andrew Carnegie.

Carnegie's first job in Allegheny was as a bobbin boy in a weaver's shop, where he worked every day but the Sabbath, for half of each day, making a little over a dollar a week. (His father was employed at the same shop, paid the same wages.) Soon he was working in the factory's boiler room, remembering that "I found myself night after night, sitting up in bed trying the steam gauges, fearing at one time that the steam was too low and that the workers above would complain that they had not power enough, and at another time that the steam was too high and that the boiler might burst." A year later, he was the telegraph operator for the local office of the Ohio Railroad Company. By 1853, he was a telegraph operator for the Pennsylvania Railroad Company, making four times what he had at his first job. A year after that he was superintendent of the western division of the corporation. Only making the equivalent of $42,000 dollars (as adjusted for inflation), the position put the gregarious, gnomish Scotsman in connection with powerful figures in the local railroad industry, then one of the most lucrative businesses in a nation rapidly expanding westward.

By the Civil War, his former employer at the Pennsylvania Railroad Company, Thomas Scott, was the new assistant secretary of war, and he charged Carnegie with the task of reopening cut rail lines into an increasingly fortified Washington, DC, precariously sitting on the border between North and South. From nearby Pittsburgh, Carnegie was able to supervise the building of a railroad encircling the capital, ensuring the arrival of thousands of federal troops into the city. Some of those battalions were led by European refugees, the radicals who'd lost in 1848. It was an auspicious, if under-commented, aspect of Carnegie's career, but one that set a template for his ambition and explained his ability to strike at the right moment.

It was by investing in needed iron munitions for the Union war cause that Carnegie first entered the industry that he'd be most indelibly connected with. From railroads, Carnegie was able to move into petroleum, and then iron and steel. With the Bessemer converter's adoption by Carnegie Steel (later US Steel), the industrialist would build an empire of iron. His immense wealth eventually rivaled that of the European monarchs whom the '48 revolutionaries had fought against. Yet with the assurance of being a pharaoh who thinks he's a prophet, Carnegie could thunder without irony that "No idol is more debasing than the worship of money!" He formed a fully-fledged philosophy of philanthropy, giving away his fortune to hospitals and colleges, foundations for world peace and tolerance, museums and concert halls, and most of all, libraries. Nowhere was his influence more marked than in Pittsburgh, where his workers could go to a Carnegie library, listen to concerts in a Carnegie music hall, and if they were lucky enough, attend a Carnegie university—even as they had difficulty joining a union at a Carnegie steel mill.

Nasaw writes that the archive does not "support the telling of a heroic narrative of an industrialist who brought sanity and rationality to an immature capitalism plagued by runaway competition, ruthless speculation, and insider corruption." The biographer adds, however, that "Nor do they support the recitation of another muckraking expose of Gilded Age criminality. The history . . . is too complex to be encapsulated in Whiggish narratives of progress or post-Edenic tales of declension, decline, and fall."

Americans pride themselves on rags-to-riches myths, but Carnegie actually lived one. When he first worked in Allegheny, he made a dollar a week. By the end of his life he'd amassed the equivalent of $372 billion dollars. If the proletariat hadn't inherited the Earth, a proletarian had.

A Nativist in Market Square

During the late 1840s, the Reverend Joseph Barker used to preach in Market Square. Clad entirely in black (sometimes with a cape and top hat) and shouting obscenity and invective, the minister sermonized against the Irish and German immigrants, overwhelmingly Roman Catholic, who were making their homes in the slums of Pittsburgh. For Barker, the United States was a nation for white, Protestant men of English stock, and the arrival of Catholics into Pittsburgh couldn't be countenanced (even though the minister's own wife was born in Ireland). He was arrested three times, once for inciting a riot in front of St. Paul's Cathedral, then located at the corner of Fifth Avenue and Grant Street.

In November 1849, Barker was arrested for the third time, on charges of having engaged in "indecent, lewd, and immoral language calculated to deprave the morals of the community" while preaching in Market Square, for which he received a sentence of a $250 fine and a year in prison. At the arraignment, Barker declared of the judge, "Now let him touch me if he dares. I'll hang him to a lamppost if he lays a finger on me." While Barker's threat may have seemed empty, Judge Patton had reason to not be so sanguine, even if he wouldn't be hung from a lamppost. In 1850, Barker led a vociferous write-in mayoral campaign, beating both the Democratic and Whig candidates under the banner of the "People's and Anti-Catholic Party," and becoming Pittsburgh's seventeenth mayor. The sentencing judge himself was the one to pardon the preacher and administer the oath of office, supposedly from the jail.

Nativist bigotry was common in the antebellum United States, embodied by the electoral success of the Know Nothing Party, which advocated against Catholics and immigrants. Maura Jane Farrelly writes in *Anti-Catholicism in America, 1620–1860* that members of the Know Nothings were "convinced that the pope was using Catholic immigrants to destroy America; for that reason alone, they fought to bar immigrants from ever holding office, restrict the number of immigrants who could come into the country in a given year, and extend the amount of time that it took before an immigrant could become a voting American citizen." Presumably, this line of thought reflected the "substance" of Barker's sermons, or worse.

Pittsburghers would soon learn what it meant to have a nativist demagogue as their leader. From the beginning of his one-year term, Mayor Barker was embroiled in controversy, criminal and otherwise. The presumable respectability of the office did nothing to temper his public tantrums. His administration was sullied by corruption, culminating in the creation of a separate police force answerable only to Barker (which was later disbanded by a judge). Pittsburgh's Catholic community feared violent attacks, and armed guards of parishioners often stood sentinel outside of churches. The mayor often came into political conflict with the stolid first bishop of the Roman Catholic Diocese, Father Michael O'Connor. Barker had both the bishop and the Mother Superior of Mercy Hospital arrested under the guise that their sewer line wasn't properly installed. Standing for reelection in 1851, Barker's histrionics were far less popular when the citizens were paying attention. He failed to even crack a quarter of the vote, and though he spent the next decade trying to win public office again, Barker would lose every contest.

David H. Bennett explains in *The Party of Fear: The American Far Right from Nativism to the Militia Movement* that "as the Know Nothing fires burned throughout large sections of America in the pre-Civil War years, dominating the political scene in major cities and states and coloring the social life of a decade, the movement marked neither the beginning nor the end of the image of America as a threatened paradise." Barker, it would seem, is one of those things that happens from time to time, which any moral citizen must remain vigilant against. His vision, if we can even use that word, was an insular, provincial, small-minded understanding of what it meant to be an American. Confronted with change, true to his name, Barker answered with a shout, trumpeting bigotry. Barker's end was just as inglorious; stumbling back to his Manchester home in 1862, the former preacher and mayor fell onto the train tracks and was decapitated by an oncoming locomotive, the only elected politician to ever be killed in such a manner. A century and a half later, Barker's hometown of Pittsburgh is tied with New York City and Boston as being among the most Catholic in the United States.

1856

The Birth of the Grand Old Party

A new political party, composed of disaffected Whigs who opposed the westward expansion of slavery as enacted by the Kansas-Nebraska Act, held their first national nominating convention in 1856. First drawing among the Yankee migrants to the Great Lakes region, and founded two years before at a meeting held in a Wisconsin schoolhouse, the new party held their inaugural national convention in Pittsburgh for the express purpose of announcing their arrival on the political stage. In a city that was controlled by a Democratic Party machine, and where even today voter registration is so blue that their primary is treated as the general election, there is a certain irony in the fact that the Republican Party was born in downtown Pittsburgh. Lewis L. Gould reflects in *The Republicans: A History of the Grand Old Party* that, concerning the participants at the Pittsburgh convention, "for all their lapses into racial prejudice, political equivocation, and poor judgement on specific aspects of the sectional crisis, the Republican Party was on the right side of the historical argument in the 1850s and their opponents were not."

A February 23 edition of the *Pittsburgh Post-Gazette* quotes the celebrated New York journalist Horace Greeley, who was a delegate to the convention. "My apprehensions are dark," said Greeley. "I know that Jefferson Davis, an implacable hater of the free State policy, is at the head of the War Department." On the eve of civil war, Greeley had every reason to fear the future Confederate "president." The Republicans' nominated candidate for the presidency, John C. Fremont, would go on to lose to the former Pennsylvanian Senator, James Buchanan, who through incompetence and political malfeasance, set the conditions that would lead to disunion. Third-party challenges are notoriously difficult in US history, and as a gathering of avowed abolitionists, the Republican Party would seem in many ways a dead-start on the national stage. Yet, four years after the drafting of an antislavery platform in Lafayette Hall at the corner of Fourth and Wood, Abraham Lincoln would take the oath of office underneath the unfinished dome of the Capitol building, awaiting its curved wrought-iron girders from Pittsburgh.

Lincoln only traveled through Pittsburgh once, as the president-elect made his way from Illinois to Washington in February 1861. From the balcony of the Monongahela House on Smithfield Street, Lincoln gave an impromptu speech from the urging of the crowd, playing to the sympathies of the audience by declaring that Pittsburgh was "widely known as the 'banner county' of the State, if not the whole Union." Despite the worsening situation in the South, as several states held successful secession votes, the president-elect still struck a tone as if reconciliation would be possible. Mayor George Wilson introduced him by calling Lincoln the "chief magistrate of our nation . . . [and] a harbinger of peace to our distracted country." Two months later, the Confederate traitors would fire on Fort Sumter, and two years later, the Confederacy would invade Pennsylvania.

Apocryphal legend holds that so ferocious were the explosions at Gettysburg, so loud the artillery and so violent the canons, that Pittsburghers heard the fighting from hundreds of miles away. Such legends underscore the precarious position of Pennsylvania, the southernmost of Northern states, on the front lines of the Civil War in the ways that New England couldn't be. Panic and fear gripped the Commonwealth, especially in Harrisburg, as news of Robert E. Lee's crossing of the Mason-Dixon Line spread and residents abandoned the capital. Pittsburgh already functioned as the US War Department's arsenal, the city instrumental to the industrial superiority of the Union, and men from throughout the Three Rivers area took up arms. Andrew Masich writes in his foreword to Len Barcousky's *Civil War Pittsburgh: Forge of the Union* that "Smoking foundries and forges worked day and night, turning out the largest iron cannons ever cast—innovations that world powers could not duplicate." Pittsburgh was only 150 miles from Gettysburg, and Masich explains that "the threat of attack and sabotage was real enough that factory workers and citizens excavated fortifications on the high ground surrounding the city." Over twenty-four rudimentary fortifications would be built in western Pennsylvania in anticipation of the invasion— ten within the city itself.

Nearly a year before Gettysburg, on the day that Union and Confederate forces met at Antietam in Maryland, a series of accidental explosions occurred at the Allegheny Arsenal, the factory which produced over 40,000 Union bullets a day, and over fourteen million in a year. The *Pittsburgh Post* reported that "So great was the force of the explosion that fragments from the laboratory were thrown hundreds of feet. . . . Shreds of clothing were found in treetops." Those who heard the blast assumed that the South had invaded Pittsburgh. Though a military investigation was convened, and some blamed the arsenal commander, Colonel John Symington, for his lax standards, the final report concluded that the "cause of the explosion could not be satisfactorily ascertained." No washerwoman to blame this time.

Regardless of the cause, the result was the single-worst civilian disaster of the war; seventy-eight workers killed who were almost entirely young women conscripted into service. The report from the *Pittsburgh Post* gives a sense of the grim intimacy of the site, observing that "The ground about was strewn with fragments of charred wood, torn clothing, bails, caps, grape shot, exploded shells, shoes, fragments of dinner baskets belonging to the inmates, steel springs from the girls' hoop skirts, cartridge paper, sheet iron, melted lead." It was impossible to identify the remains of the vast majority of the dead.

Fenian Raids

In 1866, Pittsburgh was where it was decided that the Irish would invade Canada. Founded by the Irish Republicans John O'Mahony and Michael Doheny, most who gathered at the meeting of what was known as the Fenian Brotherhood were refugees from the hideous potato famine that had killed a million people two decades before, victims of a de facto British policy of ethnic cleansing. Most of the soldiers in the Fenian Brotherhood who assembled were also veterans of the Union cause, having fought for the emancipation of the enslaved while acquiring military training that would prove useful in their upcoming plan. Overseen by Major General "Fighting Tom" Sweeny, the Fenians believed that if an organized, tactical, strategic "invasion" of British holdings in southern Canada was launched on multiple fronts across the long border, they could force Parliament and the monarchy to acknowledge Irish independence. The Fenians drew their inspiration from Thomas Osborne Davis's "rebel song," singing, " And Ireland, long a province be / A nation once again!"

The Fenians had been battle-hardened at Shiloh and Antietam, Manassas and Gettysburg, and they were able to amass their own small arsenal to aid in their military assault. Gerald F. O'Neil writes in *Pittsburgh Irish: Erin on the Three Rivers* that "Sweeny's plan for a three-pronged assault on Canada was approved in Pittsburgh," and that the city "was a major recruitment center for the planned invasion, and the sale of Irish bonds raised a considerable amount of money. A gunboat was purchased in Pittsburgh, along with arms and ammunition." In addition to ratification of their military strategy, the Fenian Brotherhood also decided in Pittsburgh that they'd be known by an alternate name—the Irish Republican Army.

O'Neil writes that the "original plan called for two diversionary threats to Toronto—a force launched from Chicago and Cleveland and another force crossing from Buffalo. The real threat to British control over Canada was supposed to be an assault on Montreal with over sixteen thousand men." The organization and planning in Pittsburgh weren't done in secret. Newspapers throughout the country covered it, and President Andrew Johnson's administration purposefully ignored the Fenian threat to Canada, in retaliation for the tacit support given to the Confederacy by the British government. According to Donald E. Graves and John R. Grodzinski in *Fighting for Canada: Seven Battles, 1758–1945,* the Fenian plans "required at least the non-intervention of the United States government, if not its active support, and it was encouraging that both President Andrew Johnson and Secretary of State William Seward had hinted at support . . . albeit in the somewhat obscure language favored by politicians." Sweeny and O'Mahony organized on the southern side of the Canadian border, and thousands of their comrades raided New Brunswick and, most spectacularly, southern Ontario, where they were briefly victorious at the Battle of Ridgeway.

Just across the Niagara River from Buffalo, a thousand men led by Brigadier General John O'Neil met their adversaries. By the end of that June day in 1866, over a hundred men would be killed. Though the US military was aware of the advancing Fenians, they waited fourteen hours before intercepting more from crossing into Canada. As they marched, the Fenians cut telegraph wires and tore up railroad tracks, their phalanx led by a green flag with a centered golden harp, the first time that emblem was used in contemporary history. At Ridgeway, the Fenians encountered the Queen's Own Rifles of Toronto, and O'Neil was able to rout the Canadians and to occupy the town, marching on to a second battle on the northern shores of Lake Erie. There the Fenians were also victorious, though they ultimately abandoned their positions as Canadian and British regulars, far superior in number, descended on them.

There were several more skirmishes over the years, though none with the drama of Ridgeway. Peter Vronsky writes in *Ridgeway: The American Fenian Invasion and the 1866 Battle that Made Canada* that the skirmish was the "melancholy baptism of the Canadian army," concluding that "Ridgeway and the Fenian invasion were in many ways a midwife to Canadian institutional modernity and its aspirations to nationhood and union." From the battlefield at Ridgeway came new and pertinent concerns from the Canadians that the British were neither willing nor capable to fully defend them against their far more powerful neighbor to the south. In 1867, the Canadians achieved their own confederation, an independence from Great Britain that still escaped the Irish. Hence the supreme irony of that vote held earlier that year in Pittsburgh; the Fenian Brotherhood had dreamt of the independence of a nation, but accidentally secured it for Canada.

The Great Railroad Strike

When the Pennsylvania Railroad and Union Depot, situated in the Strip District, caught fire in 1877, there wasn't doubt as to its cause. Torched by railroad workers themselves, the station was immolated as one of the more spectacular events in the violent strikes that stretched from Baltimore to Pittsburgh, from West Virginia to New York, and that would be remembered by enraged and fearful robber barons as the year that communism gained a toehold in the industrial heartland of the United States.

The Great Railroad Strike didn't begin in Pittsburgh, and it wasn't contained to Pittsburgh. Labor solidarity stretched from Reading and Shamokin to Scranton and Albany, as well as Syracuse and Buffalo, but Pittsburgh was where workers would fight the hardest and where state brutality would be the most marked. For forty-five days the strikers brought commerce to a halt as the nation seemed on the verge of a full-blown socialist revolution. For a brief period, the city was in the grip of the workers, an American incarnation of the Paris Commune established by anarchists, socialists, and communists for a brief few months in 1871—or at least both detractors and supporters made that comparison. Writing with purple pen a few months after the strike ended, the St. Louis journalist J. A. Dacus opined in *Annals of the Great Strikes in the United States: A Reliable History and Graphic Description of the Causes and Thrilling Events of the Labor Strikes and Riots of 1877* that "Men remembered France, and the scenes of 1789–93, and trembled as they heard the tumult increase, and saw the mighty masses of strange, grimy men, excited by passions, dark and fearful, surging along the streets."

The upheaval started in Martinsburg, West Virginia, appropriately enough on Bastille Day. Only a few months before, the federal government betrayed the promise of Reconstruction throughout the demilitarized South. Reconstruction had enacted a radical program of racial and economic justice that went far beyond the program debated at the Pittsburgh conference in 1856. West Virginians had first rejected the slave system of their state government in Richmond, and in 1877, they rejected the system of wage slavery that increasingly dominated the economics of the Gilded Age North. A connection between the "Compromise of '77" and the federal government's violent reaction to the railroad strikes is not incidental. Noted by David O. Stowell in *Streets, Railroads, and the Great Strike of 1877,* "With Reconstruction at an end, a new era of increasing conflict between labor and capital commenced." Weeks before federal troops had been patrolling Southern states. Now, with some irony, Stowell notes that those same soldiers "massed in northern cities to help suppress rioting free white laborers and other urban residents."

President Rutherford B. Hayes was instrumental in both Reconstruction's demise and the government's reaction to the strike, and as such, he was representative of the reaction against a more emancipatory politics. Such revanchism encouraged both state-sanctioned terrorism against Black Americans in the South (leading to the Great Migration northward, which demographically altered cities like Pittsburgh), as well as the anti-labor policies formed in response to workers' rights. The strike itself was born from the deprivations of the economic slump that began in 1873, a depression that would last longer than its twentieth-century counterpart. For workers across the rapidly industrializing nation, the depression was disastrous, with the moneyed class compensating by slashing employee pay, increasing work hours, and refusing to acknowledge any labor organizations. Keeping score is easy if you're being honest, for as Pittsburgh's *National Labor Tribune* noted, "These men merely want to live—and do not want their wives and little ones to starve, which they must certainly do if they are compelled to accept the terms of the company and go to work."

A fully radicalized city government refused to enforce the dictates of either the Pennsylvania Railroad or the Baltimore and Ohio Railroad, so for the second time in Pittsburgh's history, western Pennsylvania was marched on by eastern troops, as Philadelphia's National Guard were sent to enforce capital's property rights. One journalist castigated this "insane policy of calling Philadelphia troops to quell domestic quarrel" as something that was "reprehensible beyond degree," and if Pittsburgh troops were unwilling to open fire on their neighbors, the eastern interlopers were not so placid. One robber baron gleefully said that the strikers should be fed a "rifle diet for a few days and see how they like that kind of bread." So it would be, for on July 21, those troops would kill more than four dozen Pittsburghers; in response, the strikers would burn not just the depot, but dozens of buildings, hundreds of engines, passenger and railroad cars, and thousands of freight cars owned by the railroad company, while pushing the National Guard out of the city, where they hid atop the northern hills across the Allegheny River. The *Pittsburgh Sunday Globe Extra* referred to the bloodshed as "The Lexington of the Labor Conflict."

The Harmonists north of the city wondered "whether this reign of terror marked the beginnings of the harvest-time spoken of in Scripture," while a Pittsburgh newspaper sympathetic to labor thought it "the Beginning of a Revolution . . . [which] will, in the future history of this country, be designated as the beginning of the second American Revolution, which inaugurated the independence of Labor from Capital." As it was, the events of 1877 were neither apocalypse nor revolution, but rather a faint shadow from a parallel universe where the United States could have been a genuine socialist country. As with the Paris Commune, the "rioters" were agitating not just for fair working conditions, but for the profits of their own labor. Order would be restored when federal troops were activated and sent into Pittsburgh by President Hayes, drawing the experiment to a close. "Pittsburgh and the riots neither surprised nor disturbed me," wrote novelist Mark Twain, "for when the government is a sham, one must expect such things."

If American industry with all of its totalizing enormity and might was born at the Three Rivers, then so too was the response of the workingman. The lessons of 1877 are radical ones, and so knowledge of the event is often occluded and passed over, but the impromptu strike and its solidarity were a powerful spark. Labor historian Philip Fonner says as much in *The Great Labor Uprising of 1877,* writing that it was a "social rebellion, the first assertion by a national working class of a common anger against a variety of grievances—years of brutal exploitation, and a system of industrialization which viewed the worker as little more than part of the machine. . . . It was the first real evidence of working-class collective power." An editorial in a local newspaper was more succinct, if no less astute: "Pittsburgh had taught the monopolists a lesson they will never forget."

The *Pittsburgh Platform*

In a midrash of the Babylonian Talmud, it is written that upon ascending to heaven, Moses asked the Lord about the delay in receiving the Torah: "Ruler of the Universe, who is holding back Your hand?" God explains that "There is a man who will appear at the end of several generations," a great explicator of halachic law, and that his name will be Rabbi Akiva. Care must be taken with the Hebrew letters, for from "each and every mark he will derive scores and scores of laws." His curiosity piqued, Moses asks God to show him Akiva, and so the Lord propels the prophet more than fourteen centuries into the future, when Akiva was involved in the birth of Jewish oral law. Sitting in the eighth row of Akiva's symposium, listening to rabbis parse over ever-fine interpretations of halachic law, Moses soon "had no idea what they were saying." The midrash ends with the prophet's relief, for one of Akiva's students asks for the source of a ruling, to which the rabbi responds: "It's a law of Moses from Sinai."

Talmudic understanding holds that no law is completely literal; knowledge changes, shifts, and evolves with history. The authors of the midrash conveyed that Judaism is an ever-regenerative faith, and that as history compels alterations in interpretation, a chain still connects the most modern of perspectives back to an ancient origin. One wonders what Moses would have thought had he been propelled not to second-century Judea, but rather to the Concordia Club on Stockton Street in Allegheny City, where in November 1885, a group of eighteen rabbis gathered to ratify a controversial document known as the *Pittsburgh Platform*? Founded a decade before, the Concordia Club existed "to promote social and literary entertainment among its members," serving the growing and upwardly mobile German Jewish immigrant community north of Pittsburgh, including the Kaufmann family, who would lend their name to the eponymous department store chain (and make their summer home at Frank Lloyd Wright's Fallingwater), and the experimental modernist writer Gertrude Stein, who was born in Allegheny City a decade before the *Pittsburgh Platform*.

For the Jews who were members of the Concordia Club, it allowed them use of an elegant space commensurate with their growing status even while other private establishments of Pittsburgh barred them with antisemitic membership policies. Composed mostly of worshipers at the Rodef Shalom congregation, the members of the Concordia Club found themselves at home in America, believing that the prejudice and pogroms of Europe had been left behind. Even if they were barred from the social environs of Pittsburgh's ruling Protestant elite, they could make their own parallel high society. What was required, however, was a version of Judaism that would be stripped of what they saw as ethnic and religious particularism, that abandoned the strict orthodoxy of the shtetl in favor of an enlightened New World version of the faith of their fathers. As such, the goal of the *Pittsburgh Platform* was to continue what had been called in the previous century *Haskalah*—that is, the Jewish Enlightenment that reinterpreted religion in a manner that they understood as rational and modern.

Haskalah had begun in the eighteenth century alongside the liberalizing reforms that also marked Christianity during the so-called Age of Reason. Melvin Konner explains in *Unsettled: An Anthropology of the Jews* that before the "great wave of the Enlightenment . . . few Jews had the motivation to take up secular philosophy, science, or literature; after it, the floodgates of Jewish creativity opened, not just to Jewish concerns but to the entire intellectual enterprise of the West." American Jews were not consigned to ghettoes as their coreligionists often were in eastern Europe, nor were they mandated to only pursue certain jobs. Though US institutions were far from tolerant, the degree of access into education, industry, and government was unprecedented.

The *Pittsburgh Platform* was meant to reflect that reality. The convened rabbis, including signatories like Kaufmann Kohler, Isaac Mayer Wise, and Joseph Krauskopf, endorsed a set of radical pronouncements, including a rejection of strict halacha, a denouncement of nascent Zionism, and the replacement of ritual practice with purely ethical concerns. Martin Goodman writes in *A History of Judaism* that "most of the decisions expressed in the Pittsburgh Platform which emerged at the end of the conference were far more radical" than what some of the participants even desired. Yet as the *Pittsburgh Platform* emphasizes, "We recognize in Judaism a progressive religion, ever striving to be in accord with the postulates of reason," a sentiment true whether Moses would be confused or not. From that meeting historians mark the emergence of Reform Judaism.

The tragedy of the twentieth century would disavow even the most adamant of modernizers that assimilation was an easy solution to the problem of antisemitism. Pittsburgh's Jewish community also found itself changing, as the comparatively wealthy German Jews were joined by impoverished Orthodox Jews from Poland, Russia, Hungary, Romania, Ukraine, and so on. As Allegheny City's Jews had once been barred from the social clubs of Pittsburgh's Protestant ruling class, so too were the new immigrants prohibited from membership in the Concordia Club.

The geographic locus of the community was shifting as well, from Allegheny City (which had been forcibly annexed as the North Side of Pittsburgh in 1907, a decision upheld by the Supreme Court in *Hunter v. City of Pittsburgh*) to the Hill District and later the east end communities of Highland Park and especially Squirrel Hill. The latter neighborhood would establish itself as one of the most prominent Jewish communities in the nation, with every permutation of Jewish practice represented, from the steadfastly secular to the rigidly Hasidic. Ironically, for the stipulates of the *Pittsburgh Platform*, Squirrel Hill is among the largest concentrations of Orthodox Jews in an urban community outside of New York City. If the midrash teaches anything, it's that the future can be unpredictable, for Moses and the Concordia Club alike.

The Attempted Assassination of Henry Clay Frick

Among the robber barons living at the eastern edge of the city in Point Breeze—noble Carnegie with his gospel of wealth, visionary and electric George Westinghouse, familial and wholesome H. J. Heinz, and the Mellon family with their Scottish frugality—one stood apart. The others had new money pretensions of serving the social good with their philanthropic endeavors, but only Henry Clay Frick was honest enough to revel in the rotten core of avarice that defined unregulated, predatory capitalism. This was a man for whom the editors of the *New York Tribune* saw fit to eulogize by noting that his name "was abhorrent to great numbers of his fellow citizens."

Scion of the Old Overholt Rye Company, Frick arrived in Pittsburgh from Westmoreland County at the age of twenty-one and, with a loan from the future secretary of the Treasury, Andrew W. Mellon, would found H. C. Frick and Company. A millionaire before the age of thirty, Frick dominated the coal industry, responsible for some 80 percent of the ore mined from western Pennsylvania. H. C. Frick and Company would become the primary supplier of coke to Carnegie Steel, and Frick would become the eventual chairman of that corporation, embroiled in a frequently acrimonious professional relationship with its founder. Less famous than other capitalists of the Victorian era, his biographer Kenneth Warren writes in *Triumphant Capitalism: Henry Clay Frick and the Transformation of America* that he was instrumental in the "economic and social structures of the present day . . . it is indisputable that . . . [he] contributed much to the modern situation."

While Carnegie (perhaps genuinely) believed in wealth's ability to further the common good, Frick held no such compunctions. As a board member of the South Fork Fishing and Hunting Club, Frick oversaw the lowering of a massive earthen dam so as to improve the conditions for fishing, making the dam dangerously unsafe. In 1889, the unreinforced dam contributed to massive flooding some fourteen miles away in Johnstown, with a staggering death toll of over 2,000 people. Investigating the causes of the flood, the geophysicist Neil M. Coleman concludes in *Johnstown's Flood of 1889: Power Over Truth and the Science Behind the Disaster* that "powerful men found a way to control the release and probably also the content of the investigative report," so as to deny the club's negligence, malfeasance, shoddy engineering, and ultimate culpability. Coleman writes that Frick and "the other powerful members of the South Fork Fishing & Hunting Club were men accustomed to getting whatever they wanted. They had every reason to try to protect their reputations by influencing the timing of the release and conclusion" of the official report. Frick's biography is a litany of getting away with things.

By 1892, as chairman of Carnegie Steel, Frick availed himself of his business associate's vacation in Scotland to order 300 members of the Pinkerton National Detective Agency to descend upon striking steelworkers at the Homestead Steel Works. Labor historian David P. Demarest writes in *The River Ran Red* that for observers, the strike constituted a "continuing drama of working-class struggle . . . [where] the Homestead Lockout was about democratic citizenship: How would, how should America be governed?" Demarest explains that the union understood their activism as a continuation of the radical cause of that other Union during the Civil War, using metaphors of "'freemen,' 'wage slavery' and 'tyrant' industrialists. They argued that the Fricks and Carnegies of the Gilded Age were establishing a feudalism of corporate control, an aristocracy of wealth that supplanted the American ideals of democracy and participation." In the ensuing battle along the Monongahela River, nine workers and seven agents would be killed.

For travesties such as this, Frick had a reputation among reformers, progressives, and radicals as an enemy of equality. As one song popular among Slovak laborers had it, "Be firm like steel, true to the cause / And conquer Tyrant Frick." Such was the spirt that led a twenty-two-year-old Lithuanian anarchist (and lover of notorious radical Emma Goldman) named Alexander Berkman to try to assassinate Frick during the middle of the strike in the sweltering summer of 1892. Berkman stormed into Frick's downtown office and shot the capitalist at point-blank range twice in the neck, then stabbed him four times in the leg.

For the press in the city, there was relief that it wasn't a Homestead man who had been responsible; journalist Arthur Burgoyne, in his account, *The Homestead Strike of 1892,* took pains to emphasize that Berkman's actions were solely the responsibility of "Emma Goldman, a Russian woman of some note as a speech maker among the Anarchists," the would-be assassin having spent "much of his time in the beer halls frequented by Anarchists and Nihilists." Berkman would be subdued in the ensuing scuffle by Frick's assistant, and would be subsequently sentenced to twenty-two years in prison for the attempted assassination. With a hint of Faustian sulphur in the air, Frick would not only survive the attack, but he'd be back working at the desk where it occurred only a week later.

There is something of the allegory here, something Manichean—yet who was the angel and who was the devil depends on your politics. If the Gilded Age was a time of rapacious capitalism, then Berkman and Goldman represented a profound response to those depredations of business. Historian Paul Krause argues in *The Battle for*

Homestead, 1880–1892: Politics, Culture, and Steel that the "lockout became part of the lore of industrial America. It entered popular culture as a quasi-mythical epic that pitted the aspirations of organized labor against the heartless rule of greedy tyrants." Berkman would ultimately be pardoned after fourteen years, transferred from the Western Penitentiary to the Allegheny Workhouse in the last year of his imprisonment, finally gaining his freedom in 1906.

Berkman writes in *What is Communist Anarchism?* that "liberty is an empty sound as long as you are kept in bondage economically." That concept meant little to Frick, who measured worth not in justice, equality, freedom, and liberty, but rather in coal, steel, copper, and increasingly, the art masterpieces he filled his east end estate, Clayton, with, and then later his massive mansion on New York's Fifth Avenue. Frick absconded there in 1905, the environment in Pittsburgh increasingly hostile to the industrialist, even as he'd later be remembered as a proud native son. Carnegie and Frick would have a mythic falling out with one another, in large part because Carnegie didn't abide the damage to his reputation that Frick's massacre at Homestead had caused.

The final psychic cleave between the superego that was the Scotsman and the id that was his younger associate, the contradictions of claiming capitalism has a "benevolent" side washed away by the blood-red water of the Monongahela. Frick would construct a skyscraper in downtown Pittsburgh next to Carnegie's, supposedly slightly taller so he could spit onto his diminutive former mentor. Carnegie moved to New York first, and Frick followed after, building a more impressive neoclassical mansion near the Metropolitan Museum of Art. In his appropriately titled *Meet You in Hell: Andrew Carnegie, Henry Clay Frick, and the Bitter Partnership that Changed America,* Les Standiford writes that "Even to the end, then, the two titans remained locked in combat."

Of Frick's other adversary: Berkman was reunited with Goldman following his 1906 release. Both would be deported in 1919 to Russia, then in the midst of the Bolshevik Revolution, both would become victims of the US government's Anarchist Exclusion Act. At first, they enthused over the Bolsheviks, only to grow disillusioned by the Soviet Communists. By coincidence, Berkman would learn of Frick's death from a heart attack while attending a farewell banquet in Chicago; the anarchist quipped that he may have been deported by the government, but Frick had been "deported by God." Frick in New York and Berkman in Chicago—one dead and one alive, one a capitalist and one an anarchist—but both surrounded by man-made urban canyons constructed from Pittsburgh steel.

Carnegie International

Pablo de Sarasate is emergent from the purest blackness. Of delicate feature, slight build, and narrow shoulders, his thick black mustache belying the effeteness of dark curls falling onto his olive forehead. His eyes are sad, and there is a red plump to his feminine lip. With dignified confidence, the Spanish musician holds the violin, which was his partner in being one of the most celebrated interpreters of Romantic music during the late Victorian era. Elegant in fitted tuxedo, the whiteness of his starched shirt and tie propel de Sarasate into the spectator's field of vision; his two leather bluchers stand out against an undifferentiated brown surface upon which the violinist stands (unclear as to whether it's the ground or a floor), while he coalesces out of the abstracted blackness that surrounds him.

De Sarasate is as a self-creation *ex nihilo,* as if all of the swirling particles of chaos have momentarily seen fit to collect into the form of this slender, delicate, beautiful man. The overall effect for the viewer of the celebrated painter James Abbott McNeill Whistler's oil painting, *Arrangement in Black: Portrait of Señor Pablo de Sarasate,* standing a little over six feet tall and a blazingly modern combination of the figurative and the abstract, is as if being privy to witnessing some vampiric immortal conjure himself from the ether. The rarefied elegance to Whistler's masterpiece stands in stark contrast to the grit of Pittsburgh, but it shares in that blackness of the mill's exhaust pumping out every hour of the day beyond the doors of the Department of Fine Arts of the Carnegie Institute, which purchased the painting in 1896.

This was the beginning of what would be called the Carnegie Museum of Art, housed at the time in a room of Carnegie's most magnificent library, constructed on Forbes Avenue in the increasingly fashionable neighborhood of Oakland. By 1896, the city was the eleventh largest in the United States, with a population of well over 300,000 (less than half of its height some five decades later, yet more than today). Carnegie wasn't the only philanthropist anxious that his status as new money wouldn't avail him of the proper respect amongst the eastern aristocracy, and so in a flurry of construction, Oakland was to become the cultural center of America's industrial powerhouse.

A few years before, the wealthy landowner Mary Schenley donated 300 acres for a public park planned according to the principles of stewardship exemplified by figures like landscaper Frederick Law Olmsted, including the extensive Phipps Botanical Gardens. By the early 1890s, Carnegie intended to add to Schenley's gift, and to request an additional hundred acres for his institution, writing to his board president that the "best way to present the matter to her . . . is to show that the ground is absolutely necessary to make the Park she has given available." Carnegie's vision for Oakland was in keeping with the sentiment that Oakland "would soon be the residential center of the city, connected by horsecar and trolley with downtown," as Nasaw writes.

Schenley's gift inaugurated Oakland as the de facto academic, cultural, and leisure hub of Pittsburgh; from her generosity would come institutions like the Western Pennsylvania Institution for the Blind, the exhibition of public art, fountains, and gardens, and commercial space to be used for apartment buildings and businesses. Such a project kept with the eventual mission of the *Pittsburgh Survey,* conducted in 1906–7 by the Russell Sage Foundation so as to suggest issues of reform that could improve the city's standard of living.

Maurine Weiner Greenwald and Margo J. Anderson explain in *Pittsburgh Surveyed: Social Science and Social Reform in the Early Twentieth Century* that a conclusion of that landmark study was that "In place of the dirty, exploitative world they investigated, the surveyors proposed that Pittsburghers strive to create a community with safer work environments, clean water, clear air, open space, decent housing, and a higher standard of living for workers and their families."

In a matter of a few years, Oakland was home to the Carnegie Institute of Technology, founded in 1900. In 1905, Luna Park would become the first amusement park to entertain guests by using only electric lights. The Roman Catholic Diocese would move St. Paul's Cathedral into a magnificent gothic structure on Fifth Avenue in 1906, and the University of Pittsburgh would relocate its campus from the North Side to Oakland in 1909. A baseball stadium for the Pittsburgh Pirates called Forbes Field would open that same year, and the Arabesque-styled Syria Mosque became home to the Pittsburgh Symphony Orchestra in 1911. The Mellon Institute for scientific research commenced operations in 1913.

Soon, the stately, federal and neoclassical-style neighborhood, with its blocks of long monumental buildings, including the Pittsburgh Athletic Association, the Masonic Temple, the University Club, and the Soldiers and Sailors Memorial Hall for the veterans of the Grand Army of the Republic, became one of the most magnificent districts in the Northeast. Architectural librarian Martin Aurand writes in *The Spectator and the Topographical City* that "within the rich urban fabric of Pittsburg's Oakland district, is one of the great, albeit little known and not fully realized, sites of American architecture, landscape, and urbanism," a triumph of the City Beautiful Movement.

No institution would be more prominent than the jewel of Carnegie's philanthropic campaign, his massive institute that housed the largest library of the 2,509 that he built throughout the world, a concert hall, a natural history museum, where he assembled the second-largest collection of dinosaurs (his great passion) in the United States, and the art museum. Carnegie had no intention of spending inordinate amounts of his fortune on medieval and Renaissance masterpieces. Instead, he opted to purchase massive plaster casts of architectural marvels throughout the world, common practice in the late nineteenth and early twentieth centuries, to assemble imitation sculptures, with the museum's collection remaining among the finest. For painting, Carnegie felt it pragmatic to purchase the "Old Masters of Tomorrow," and so in 1896, he inaugurated the Carnegie International, a comprehensive exhibition of contemporary art held every four years as a "Chronological Collection, intended to represent the progress of painting in America, beginning with the year 1896."

The Carnegie International predated the Whitney Biennial by thirty-six years, and the Carnegie Museum of Art established itself thirty-three years before New York's Museum of Modern Art. From Carnegie's frugality, there was a fortuitous daring that established the first modern art museum in the world. Carnegie was disappointed by the national press's indifference to the International, complaining that there had not been "the slightest mention in any of the papers" the morning the gallery opened, for the "public sentiment is all right in Pittsburgh, but it now remains to bring the Exhibition before the country."

The Carnegie International has arguably never received its full acclaim, for behind the granite façade of the museum, with its bronze statues of Michelangelo, Shakespeare, Bach, and Galileo representing art, literature, music, and science, there was an exhibition as forward-thinking as anything in New York. Over the next century, Americans would be introduced by the International to Winslow Homer, Camille Pissarro, Pablo Picasso, Salvador Dali, Rene Magritte, Willem de Kooning, Jackson Pollock, and native Pittsburghers Mary Cassatt and Andy Warhol. In its own unassuming way, Pittsburgh was able to quietly give shape to the zeitgeist.

A lesser-known artist who first made his appearance at the 1927 Carnegie International was a self-taught painter and Scottish-born Irish immigrant named John Kane, who lived among the steep rowhouses of working-class Greenfield. Kane was a paragon of what's termed "outsider art"—that is, nonacademic compositions from artists without formal training. Inheritor of Pittsburgh's earthy, Old World Roman Catholicism, Kane's vision was one that saw transcendence as imbuing even the most profane of material with a sacred luminescence. His most famous painting places liturgical drama directly in Oakland itself. Art historian Franklin Toker writes in *Pittsburgh: A New Portrait* that Kane's "most iconic image of Pittsburgh is the Pieta painted in 1933 . . . [setting] Mary's lamentation over the body of Christ in the middle of Oakland. You can easily make out the . . . Carnegie Institute, and St. Paul's Cathedral in the background." Kane replaced Jerusalem with Pittsburgh, depicting holiness's presence within the present, and the intrinsic beauty of every sacred moment.

Such are the temples we build, even amidst grime, soot, and grit.

PART III

A CONSEQUENCE OF AMERICA

Rise, Fall, and Reinvention

(1900–)

The Red Velvet Swing

Stanford White fucked the model Evelyn Nesbit on his red velvet swing. For that reason, her eventual husband—Pittsburgh coal baron Harry Kendall Thaw—would confront White at New York's Madison Square Garden in June 1906. There, the psychotically jealous Thaw would shoot and murder the architect White in front of thousands of people seated in a building designed by the latter. Readers thrilled to pulpy yellow journalism detailing White's murder and Thaw's conviction in the subsequent "Trial of the Century," the first mass-media spectacle that made a brutal domestic tragedy into entertainment. In Thaw's trial, all of the combustible obsessions of the Gilded Age—decadent wealth, hideous inequity, and sexual exploitation—would be displayed on the front pages of America's newspapers. As contemporary journalist Alfred Henry Lewis wrote, "A rich man has been killed, a rich man did the killing, and so a world sits up to hear the tale in every red and dripping particular."

Even more intoxicating was Nesbit, and the perceived role she had in supposedly driving her husband to murderous madness. Paula Uruburu writes in *American Eve: Evelyn Nesbit, Stanford White, the Birth of the "It" Girl and the Crime of the Century* how the Pittsburgh that the model was born into was one where those "unfortunate enough to have to scrape out a living in the deep choking cramp of the steel mills and coal mines were also forced to inhabit ramshackle row houses that weren't much better than the dark holes they toiled in for pennies a day." Nesbit's almost supernatural beauty afforded a degree of both salvation and damnation, as she became a commodity fought over by powerful men, moving from the rowhouses of Tarentum to the brownstones of Manhattan and Pittsburgh's Millionaire's Row, where Uruburu writes, "imposing mansions and mock-English gardens sat podgy and stodgy and secure behind colonnades of trees, enormous boxwood hedges, and decorative gilded gates."

A chorus girl who was among the first young women to become widely known in the pinup industry, Nesbit was born in bleak, working-class Tarentum on Christmas Day in 1885, making her life later in Philadelphia and New York. Known for her preternatural beauty, the delicate, pale-skinned Nesbit, with her cascade of auburn hair, was a favored model for photographers, painters, and illustrators, performing on Broadway, which led to her meeting White. The architect maintained a reputation for talent, but also for his dalliances, his unrepentant bisexuality, and his apartment above the high-end toy store, FAO Schwartz, on West Twenty-Fourth Street. There, he maintained a mirror-paneled sex room where White—architect of Washington Square Park's triumphal arch, the Boston Public Library at Copley Square, and the Rosecliff Estate in Newport, Rhode Island—would first rape Nesbit. It was for that traumatic event, and the subsequent consensual sexual relationship that it led to, that Thaw would murder White.

Writing in *My Story,* Nesbit explained that "White was a member of a small clique of men who had vicious tendencies . . . performed frequently without remorse, with the sense that he and his friends were immune to the laws of the land." The tragedy of Nesbit's life was that her clear-eyed knowledge of these arrangements could do little to prevent her abuse at the hands of similar sociopaths, one of whom would be her husband, Thaw. That prince of the Pittsburgh ruling class, born to the coal maven William Thaw Sr., could match White in narcissism, sociopathy, addiction, and sadism, even while

Thaw couldn't match the architect's talent. Known for his infatuation for prostitutes, Thaw was expelled from Harvard and relied on his father's connections to save him from prosecution for the violent acts he committed.

Thaw was obsessed with Nesbit, who was performing in *The Wild Rose* on Broadway, which he attended forty times. By charming Nesbit's vulnerable family, Thaw was able to badger her into accepting a marriage proposal, though the possibility of extricating herself from White was undoubtedly part of the appeal. Thaw, for all of his own promiscuity, was obsessed with female chastity, and he pressured Nesbit into revealing all of the details of her sexual relationship with White. While traveling in Europe, Thaw repeatedly sexually assaulted his fiancée, writing in a visitor's log at the site of Joan of Arc's martyrdom that the saint "would not have been a virgin if Stanford White had been around." At their 1905 wedding, Thaw demanded that Nesbit wear a black dress with brown trim.

Thaw was increasingly paranoid that White was privately mocking him, the former feeling acutely a type of class embarrassment that only the very rich are capable of, worrying that as new money, he'd never be recognized among New York's moneyed elite. If Nesbit was known as the "Pittsburgh peach," then Thaw's squished features had White referring to the socialite as the "Pennsylvania pug." Thaw made his decision to kill White, and did so at the conclusion of an outdoor performance of the musical *Mam'zelle Champagne.* The playboy jumped forward, screamed something, and fired at point-blank range, tearing off the entire lower portion of White's face and burning what remained to a cinder black. Witnesses at the trial couldn't agree as to whether Thaw had shouted "You ruined my wife!" or "You ruined my life!"

As with subsequent "trials of the century," the Thaw conviction had less to do with crime than it did with the sheer, thrilling spectacle. Readers of headlines like "Woman Whose Beauty Spelled Ruin and Death" cared little for Nesbit, titillated rather by sex and death. Imprisoned in Manhattan's infamous Tombs, Thaw was allowed to eat Delmonico's and drink champagne every night, retiring to a brass bed. His attorneys argued innocence by reason of temporary insanity, claiming that his was an act of chivalry. After two trials, Thaw would be remanded to a mental institution. Thaw divorced Nesbit upon his release in 1915, dying in Miami three decades later. Nesbit outlived him by twenty years. Having been the abused possession of two rich men for the better part of the twentieth century, her infamy and trauma sustained a career in vaudeville, burlesque, and then Hollywood. Overcoming struggles with alcohol and morphine, she died in 1967. Her last few years were happy, working incongruously as a ceramics instructor.

The beautiful girl on the red velvet swing was only ever an enigma because nobody ever thought to ask what Nesbit thought about anything. Denied her agency, the chorus girl had to survive as she could, whether near the coal mines of Tarentum, the steel mills of Pittsburgh, or the penthouses of New York. Any society so dedicated to the proposition that inequity should be universal can't help but make drama cheap and tragedy tawdry, the violence that men enact on women and each other turned into entertainment. Uruburu writes that Nesbit's "life after that ghastly night and the trials that followed continued to move along in fits and starts, capturing in brief but vivid flashes an America always deliriously teetering on the brink of self-awareness. Or self-annihilation."

Maybe it wasn't the murder that inaugurated our age, but a different event which occurred only a few miles from Thaw's mansion on Pittsburgh's Fifth Avenue, when Harry Davis and John Harris opened an establishment on Smithfield Avenue. Drawing the name of their storefront from a portmanteau combining the price of admission and the Greek word for "theater," Davis and Harris would call their business a "nickelodeon"—the first establishment devoted exclusively to showing movies. By the time of White's murder, nickelodeons in the style of Pittsburgh's original had proliferated across the country.

That summer, one of the most popular films was a dramatization of the Nesbit affair produced by Thomas Edison entitled *Rooftop Murder*—so popular that it would push *The Story of Jesus* out of marquees. Released a week after White had been shot, *Rooftop Murder* was as popular as it was because of the rumor that Nesbit played herself. She didn't—though she'd be the technical adviser for 1955's *The Girl in the Red Velvet Swing,* where Joan Collins dramatized her traumas. (Another doomed ingenue, Marilyn Monroe, had refused the role.)

"The tragedy wasn't that Stanford White died," Nesbit later wrote, "but that I lived."

The Pittsburgh Agreement

By the spring of 1918, it was inevitable that the Austro-Hungarian Empire would collapse. That hodgepodge quilt of ethnicities, nationalities, languages, and religions ruled by the Hapsburg aristocracy from Vienna was to be a casualty of having fought on the losing side in the First World War. Author Simon Winder describes this defunct country in *Danubia: A Personal History of Habsburg Europe,* noting that it was "complex, multilingual, religiously diverse, experimental and self-confident." While the Hapsburgs exemplified a profoundly conservative world, an aristocracy built upon a rigidly hierarchical and bureaucratic central state, Austria-Hungary's diversity still posed a certain model of liberal multiculturalism.

Winder quips that the Austro-Hungarian Empire was a "plural, anarchic, polyglot Europe once supervised in a dizzying blend of ineptitude, viciousness and occasional benignity by the Habsburg family." Now, in the autumn of empire, a little more than two dozen men who were previously subjects of the Hapsburgs gathered at the main hall of a fraternal organization with the unlikely name of the Loyal Order of Moose on Penn Avenue in downtown Pittsburgh, and they drafted a declaration that was to delineate and define into existence an entirely new country named Czechoslovakia.

The Loyal Order of Moose was to be the Independence Hall of the newly declared nation, for that was where (with support from the administration of President Woodrow Wilson) "the Pittsburgh Agreement" was to be signed by representatives of several different Czech and Slovak expat fraternal organizations. Led by Tomáš Garrigue Masaryk, who a few months later would govern from Prague as the country's first president, the Pittsburgh Agreement promised to "bring about a Union of the Czechs and Slovaks in an independent state comprising the Czech Lands . . . and Slovakia." In a region long split by linguistic, ethnic, and religious differences, for which an enduring peace had been established for generations by the Hapsburgs, the authors of the Pittsburgh Agreement vowed that the "Czecho-slovak state will be a republic, its Constitution will be democratic."

Masaryk was a liberal, a humanist, a rationalist, a secularist, and a student of the eighteenth-century Enlightenment, and with his fellow countrymen, such as the priest Jozef Murgaš, the leader of the Bohemian National Alliance Vojta Beneš, and journalist Karel Pergler, he desired to ensure the establishment of a Czechoslovakian republic that embodied modern values. "America meant more to Masaryk than the powerful, prosperous country whose entry into the war turned the scales in favor of the Allies," writes George J. Kovtun in *Masaryk and America: Testimony of a Relationship,* for the patriot "regarded America as a *spiritual* force . . . he now saw more clearly than before the basic similarities between American traditions and the democratic aspirations of oppressed European nations."

From the sprawling, confusing, expansive territory of what had once been Austro-Hungary, the disparate ethnicities of the soon-to-be former empire would come to establish individual nation-states. Immigrants from Austria-Hungary who settled in the United States were compelled by the US government to choose either "Austrian" or "Hungarian" as their primary ethnicity, even as the reality of the central European empire was more complicated than that. Pittsburgh, like other cities in the industrial Midwest, became a locus for immigrants from the Hapsburg lands, who labored in factories and mills. Before the signatories of the Pittsburgh Agreement gathered at the Loyal Moose Hall, they'd previously met in Chicago and Cleveland, a reflection of their demographic breadth. In addition to the German-speaking Austrians and Magyar-speaking Hungarians, Austria-Hungary was also home to Romanians, Bosnians, Albanians, Serbians, Italians, Poles, Carpatho-Rusyns, Ukrainians, Czechs, and Slovaks— with immigrants from soon-to-be-independent nations finding new homes in the steep neighborhoods of Pittsburgh. Several of these ethnic and linguistic groups already identified with larger nations to whom they understood themselves as being repatriated toward; others, with a sense of Romantic nationalism that owed much to the thought of the previous century, dreamt of the resurrection of kingdoms that in some cases hadn't existed for generations.

Nor would the constructed and imagined state of Czechoslovakia exist for that long, either. Masaryk would die three years before the Munich Agreement ensured the Nazi occupation of the Sudetenland, and a decade before the Soviet Union would extend its sphere of influence over Prague, violently putting down the democratic rebellion of 1968. Masaryk's dreams were of a constitutional, democratic republic, but tiny Czechoslovakia would be pressed between totalitarian nightmares of fascism and Stalinism. Mary Heimann writes in *Czechoslovakia: The State that Failed* that the nation has often been understood as "a country with deeply rooted humane, liberal and democratic values that was twice betrayed: first, in 1938, by its Western allies, and again, in 1968, by its eastern neighbors." A cautionary tale, for "it shows how nationalism, even in a democratic country, could move seamlessly from democracy through Fascism."

Though small and beleaguered, Czechoslovakia would have an outsize influence on world letters as the home of Franz Kafka, Milan Kundera, and Václav Havel. The last of these was the playwright who'd be elected to Masaryk's old position, albeit after the Pittsburgh Agreement was nullified in 1993. That was the year that the Velvet Revolution concluded, a nonviolent rebellion against Communist rule that saw the Czech and Slovak Republics peacefully separating. In the bloodless dissolution of these two states, Czechoslovakia had demonstrated a certain humane, liberal toleration that was so valorized by Masaryk and the other authors of the Pittsburgh Agreement, but ironically only through the sacrifice of that nation itself.

A Cathedral of Learning

Though he was a stolid, Iowa-born midwesterner, Chancellor John Gabbert Bowman of the University of Pittsburgh still had an educator's understanding of how spectacle has pedagogical import. Such was the flamboyance that Bowman exhibited when he convened a group of Pittsburgh civic and business leaders at Oakland's University Club in 1924, overlooking the neighborhood which had increasingly taken on the appearance of Athens's Acropolis. From the southern windows of the club, diagonal from an empty plot of green space called Frick Acres, Bowman asked the assembled audience to visualize a rather different structure than what already existed, what he had described in private writings a few years before as a "high building, a tower—a tower singing upward that would tell the epic story of Pittsburgh."

To those at the dinner, Bowman presented a granite disk cored from deep within the earth underneath Frick's Acre, a plot of land donated to the university by the Mellon family on which the chancellor intended to construct his masterpiece. The disks were to be both a paperweight souvenir for the potential donators but also a demonstration that the ground was solid enough to support Bowman's anticipated fifty-story skyscraper, intended to be the tallest educational structure in the world. Writing in his personal papers three years before, Bowman hoped that the university's new central building would be one where students "shall find wisdom . . . and faith—in steel and stone, in character and thought—they shall find beauty, adventure, and moments of high victory." He would give the building the dreamlike name of the Cathedral of Learning.

Toker refers to it as the "still more preposterous Cathedral of Learning," calling it "the most extravagant college building in the world." And yet another argument could be made that Bowman's quixotic desire had the sublime about it, this absurd and beautiful building the architectural equivalent of Pre-Raphaelite painting or Romantic poetry. Oakland already had a distinguished landscape, with its assortment of marble columned buildings, most designed by Henry Hornbostel. The Columbia University-trained architect had a certain vision for what Pittsburgh should look like, drawing from the neoclassical rationalism of the City Beautiful movement and envisioning the city's educational and cultural corridor as being occupied by wide, long, and low buildings that would stretch on for blocks in swaths of Indiana limestone and New England granite. A representative example of Hornbostel's aesthetic would be his beaux arts masterpiece, the Soldiers and Sailors Memorial, constructed for the Grand Army of the Republic as an auditorium and museum. The structure was built according to the exact dimensions and appearance of the Mausoleum at Herculaneum—an imposing tan edifice peaked with a dark, tiled roof.

Hornbostel had similarly valorized Greco-Roman aesthetics in projects as varied as Rodef Shalom's new Fifth Avenue synagogue, the Pittsburgh City-County Building, and almost the entirety of the campus of Carnegie Tech. Bowman wanted the University of Pittsburgh to make its own distinctive mark on Oakland's skyline, and if Hornbostel was content to build out, then the chancellor wanted to build up. He would reject the staid conservatism of the Athenian neighborhood, for not only would the Cathedral of Learning be the tallest school building in the world, but the largest neo-Gothic structure as well. Perhaps as gesture to the increasingly Catholic nature of the city, the Cathedral of Learning was to have the appearance of a great medieval monastery or university, a limestone symphony of gargoyles and grotesques ascending in dozens of stories above Oakland. Bowman would write that the cathedral was to be "more than a schoolhouse; it was to be a symbol of the life that Pittsburgh . . . had wanted to live. It was to make visible something of the spirit . . . of the great city that would sometime spread out beyond their three rivers."

Ground was broken in 1926 for a design by the master neo-Gothic architect Charles Z. Klauder. "It is no accident that the architectural style of the most distinctive educational building in the world, the Cathedral of Learning, combines the modern skyscraper with the medieval Gothic cathedral," writes Robert C. Alberts in *Pitt: The Story of the University of Pittsburgh, 1787–1987.* Alberts argues that the "symbol of industrial and commercial America is thus united with the symbol of a more spiritual and contemplative . . . time and place." The eventual design put the Cathedral of Learning at forty-two stories, among the tallest skyscrapers in the world at the time and still the most grandiose of educational buildings. Klauder envisioned a massive "Common Room" flanking the entirety of the first three floors, a vaulted-ceilinged and flying-buttressed structure modeled on the naves of medieval cathedrals, with an assortment of hidden passageways, dark corridors, and alcoves scattered throughout. The final girder was put in place in 1929, a week before the stock market crash that precipitated the Great Depression.

While construction was underway during the 1920s, Bowman led a massive capital campaign to fund the building, based on the "Buy a Brick" campaign, where schoolchildren could raise money and join the "Fellowship of Builders." Over 97,000 western Pennsylvanian students contributed. In 1926, the visionary college administrator Ruth Crawford Mitchell proposed the "Nationality Rooms" project, whereby local immigrant fraternal organizations representing the increasing diversity of the booming city would design and fund classrooms representing their homelands. Such incisive financial acumen was helpful during the Depression, with the Cathedral of Learning's first class held on schedule in 1931 and the cornerstone of the Common Room put in place by 1937. Upon completion, the Cathedral of Learning soared over Hornbostel's Acropolis, the exact geographic center of Pittsburgh and Allegheny County, visible from virtually all of the city's ninety neighborhoods and the veritable symbol of the growing metropolis.

Mitchell's directorship of the Nationality Rooms deserves special commendation, for no assortment of educational spaces in the United States would be comparable to them. Conceived of as a fundraising gambit, the Nationality Rooms quickly became an assertion of dignity on behalf of the immigrant populations who were tasked with their design and completion. To this date, there are thirty rooms representing a variety of cultural groups within the city, with some of the earliest built (for the university still opens new ones, reflecting the increasing diversity of the city) including the Irish, Italian, Hungarian, Czechoslovak, Polish, Greek, German, Lithuanian, Romanian, English, Scottish, Syrian-Lebanese, and Chinese rooms.

Such was an architectural embodiment of the massive demographic changes in Pittsburgh, as immigrants flocked into the mills and neighborhoods of the city, transforming the region. Each room was to distinctively represent the cultural and educational history of an individual country; no contemporary political symbols were to be allowed, and though the university promised a room and upkeep in perpetuity, it was the responsibility of a convened committee of representatives to decide on design, funding, and construction. The guiding principle of the rooms, as inscribed on a copper plate in the Common Room, is that "they offer their gifts of

133

what is precious, genuine and their own, to truth that shines forever and enlightens all people."

A representative example would be the Italian Room, a walnut-colored space with an inset of built-in chairs that look as if they're from a Tuscan monastery, the backs of which are emblazoned in gold with the names of Italian universities and their year of founding, the earliest being Bologna in 1088. As with all of the rooms, there are original details from actual historical sites; the Italian Room includes a Florentine fireplace and a cabinet for the keeping of priestly vestments. On the back wall is a painting of Elena Lucrezia Cornaro Piscopia, who in the seventeenth century became the first woman to receive a college degree when she graduated from the University of Padua. Across from her, above the chalkboard, is a bust of the poet Dante.

By the second decade of the twentieth century, Pittsburgh had one of the largest Italian communities of any North American city, the bulk of whom immigrated from the poor, mountainous, rural province of Abruzzi. That room would be dedicated in 1949, a quarter of a century after the Reed-Johnson Act effectively banned Italian immigration to the United States and twenty-two years after Nicola Sacco and Bartolomeo Vanzetti were executed for the "crimes" of being anarchists and Italians. For those who worked in Pittsburgh's mills, the vast majority of whom had no higher education and still faced virulent discrimination, something like the Italian Room represented both dignity and pride in the past and hope and faith in the future.

The tower rises dozens of stories taller than the buildings around it, sitting like a massive golem spying out over the valleys, hills, and rivers of the city. Alberts quotes the recollection of a man from the Hill District, who would go on to earn a BA and PhD from the university. He remembers that "Each morning when I was roused by my parents . . .

one of the first things I saw out my window was the upper floors of the Cathedral of Learning. . . . My one hope, almost consuming, was that I might somehow, some way, someday, be able to go to college. . . . I knew that that was my way up and where I wanted to be." Such was the dedication in the Common Room, with its solemn promise that "Here is eternal spring; for you the very stars of heaven are new."

An Activist in the Making

Placed amongst the old mansions of Pittsburgh's Gilded Age aristocracy, the Pennsylvania College for Women (now Chatham University) sat on a bucolic hilltop straddling Shadyside and Squirrel Hill and educated generations of the daughters of Pittsburgh's establishment class. The campus was a hidden neighborhood of brick and stone, marble and stained glass, elm and ivy, a radically different reality from the mill-blackened city skies surrounding it. In January 1928, a year before the last girder at the Cathedral of Learning was rivetted into place, a PCW undergraduate from the suburb of Springdale would switch her major from English to biology. Her name was Rachel Carson, and by filing a change of major request, she initiated the contemporary environmental movement.

A reading of Carson's later works, including the "Sea Trilogy" of 1941's *Under the Sea Wind,* 1951's *The Sea Around Us,* and 1955's *The Edge of the Sea*, certainly demonstrates a prodigious talent beyond that of the typical English major. But there was something that wasn't unexpected about Carson's decision of changing majors; one of her formative memories was of a hilltop foray in Springdale, when as a young girl she'd happened across a fossilized shell from the long-ago Pennsylvanian era and wondered at how her landlocked homestead had once been on the ocean. A fortuitous decision, this change in majors, for Carson was able to marry her literary talents with her academic training, eventually receiving a master's in biology from Johns Hopkins University. The result, as Linda Lear explains in *Rachel Carson: Witness for Nature,* was a "a singular vision encompassing nothing less than the mysteriously intricate living world whose workings she understood so deeply and described for others with such power."

Silent Spring is a testament to Carson's poetic facility with language. Her 1962 treatise on the dangers of pesticides, particularly DDT, was momentously effective at policy change because of its prose. Few writers can imagine the sort of influence that Carson garnered, her book directly leading to the establishment of the Environmental Protection Agency and legislation that banned DDT. As she wrote in *Silent Spring,* "For each of us, as for the robin in Michigan or the salmon in the Miramichi, this is a problem of ecology, of interrelationships, of interdependence." Carson's prose was forged in the kiln of Pittsburgh; the disjunct between the pristineness of her Allegheny Valley youth and of Pittsburgh filth only a few miles downriver was apparent, where "We poison the caddis flies in a stream and the salmon runs dwindle and die. We poison the gnats in a lake and the poison travels from link to link of the food chain and soon the birds of the lake margins become its victims. We spray our elms and the following springs are silent of robin song." In turning away from her expected studies, Carson embraced a deeper sort of poetry written in epoch and strata, in flora and fauna, "the web of life—or death—that scientists know as ecology."

Carson's Springdale was both environmentally and spiritually distant from Pittsburgh, even if it was literally close, for as the *Pittsburgh Leader* noted in 1901, a few years before she would be born, the town was one of "considerable acreage of woods and farm land . . . set amidst overhanging apple trees and maples." She grew up in a whitewashed wood clapboard colonial home that abutted the river; Carson's views would have not been dissimilar to the same vista espied by the Indians and colonial settlers who made their way through the region two centuries before.

Within Pittsburgh, however, the continual dun of industry operating every hour of the day and all days of the week made a landscape that was an oily, dark, dirty, grimy, besotted, and coal-filled valley of concrete and brick; a city of perpetual midnight where if a house like Carson's had been placed in the midst of all this activity, it would have been stained black within a few months by all of the mill exhaust. Examine the copious early twentieth-century photographs of Pittsburgh documenting the environment, pictures taken by men like the iconic journalist Charles "Teenie" Harris, who worked for the *Pittsburgh Courier,* America's largest Black newspaper, or the photo essays of W. Eugene Smith originally intended for *Life* magazine.

What they reveal is a Pittsburgh as dark Gotham, a place where it would be pitch-black even at noon, where homes required a separate basement entrance with a shower to clean all of the soot off of your clothes before retiring upstairs. This was the ecological context of Carson's schooling when she decided that her talents lay with the life sciences rather than with stanzas and verse. Lear writes that "Pittsburgh's reputation as the iron and steel capital of the world was earned at the cost of creating the worst air and water pollution in the country," explaining that "Although PCW was located miles upriver from the Bessemer mills and the mountains of molten slag that illuminated the sky . . . the campus was not immune from the fine soot that hung in the air, penetrating the crevices of every building, stinging the eyes, nose, and mouth."

Silent Spring was, both literally and metaphorically, a product of this environment. Carson would never have written what she did if hers had only been a life of wilderness, for it was in the degradations of the polluted city that the young biologist was able to first grasp what exactly was at stake.

Joe Magarac in *Scribner's*

At any hour of the day, you could find mill workers lining up at the brass rail of the bars on East Carson Street running parallel to the Monongahela on the city's South Side. Sometimes an after-work drink (or twelve) would be at noon; sometimes it would be at the crack of dawn—whenever workers would end their shifts at the massive, almost interstellar-looking Jones and Laughlin Mill. According to an article by journalist Owen Francis, published by *Scribner's Magazine* in 1931, there was an unusual topic of conversation that was popular in the dives and fraternal clubs of the neighborhood, be it the Polish Falcons or the Slovene National Benefit Society, a discussion about a figure claimed alike by Croatian, Hungarian, Czech, and Slovak workers from J&L to the Homestead Steel Works.

Using the common derogatory slur against eastern European laborers in Pittsburgh, Francis claimed that the story was "typical of the Hunkie," a fantastic legend about prodigious feats of strength unthinkingly performed by a man more robot than human. "My name is Joe Magarac," says the being in Francis's article, "all I know is to work and eat like a donkey. I'm the only man of steel in the world." Francis's essay purported that the mill workers of Pittsburgh had their very own folk hero in this figure of "Joe Magarac," whose surname literally means "Jackass" in Hungarian. Magarac was a Pittsburgh equivalent of Paul Bunyan or John Henry, a genuine piece of oral storytelling born in the mills, bars, churches, and social organizations of Pittsburgh. In the story, Magarac is literally born from molten metal itself (his surname notwithstanding).

Magarac's birth and life are supernatural and superhuman, as is his death. Ivan Kovacevic explains in the *Journal of Folklore* that this figure who "made steel rail tracks with his bare hands" had proven "so good and fast at this that in no time there were railroad tracks everywhere in the region of the steel mill. This led to the closing of several mills for a few days." Magarac was nothing if not a creature of solidarity; distressed at how his productivity had endangered the livelihoods of his fellow workers, he comes to a radical decision. "When the steelworkers returned to the factory," Kovacevic writes, "they found Joe melting into a furnace; he explained to them how he could not get over the mill closing and that the steel into which he would melt would be the best that was ever made." And so, workers who figuratively gave their flesh to the mill told tale of an idealized version of themselves who literally did that as well.

According to Francis, Pittsburgh's eastern European laborers thrilled to the stories about the honest, hardworking, broad, and dim-witted steel worker who did the tasks of two dozen men effortlessly and never had to sleep or rest. If you were to believe the writer (who though he'd been a Hollywood screenwriter, was a Pittsburgh native who once labored in the mills himself), working for a periodical that had published Edith Wharton, Ernest Hemingway, and Theodore Roosevelt, then Pittsburgh's steelworkers uncomplicatedly told this tale over boilermakers of Canadian Club rye and Iron City beer. The difficulty with that claim is that there is no evidence of stories concerning Magarac having proliferated before the *Scribner's* article, with the most popular explanations for this deficit being that either the journalist or those interviewed had concocted the legend. Kovacevic even considers the possibility that Magarac's origins are with US Steel (the descendant of Carnegie Steel) as a bit of colorful propagandizing that would minimize friction between labor and management.

Magarac would seem to be what anthropologists call "fakelore"—that is, consciously constructed folklore. Kovacevic makes an observation, however, that "the faith of many fakelore creations shows that they went through a process of folklorisation and that they became a legitimate part of collective storytelling." In other words, even if Magarac wasn't a real folktale, the narrative was imbued by collective agency far beyond the original *Scribner's* article. The Man of Steel has become a strange Pittsburgh folkway; he appears on a mural in the Carnegie Museum of Art, all rippled muscles and ruddy skin under blond hair dappled with flop sweat while he labors over the Bessemer converter; his visage sneaks into Art Deco friezes in downtown Pittsburgh, and figures very much like him are in the federal art made by the Works Progress Administration during President Franklin Roosevelt's New Deal. He was even depicted on a ride at the Kennywood amusement park. Most spectacularly of all, sculptor Frank Vittor proposed a monumental steel statue of Magarac as part of the Renaissance I urban renewal project in 1951. Vittor imagined that at the confluence of the rivers there could be a hundred-foot-tall statue of a muscular Magarac rendered by the aesthetic conventions of socialist realism, holding two fountains meant to look like ladles propelling water into a third stream, all colored with lights to imitate the orange glow of molten steel.

There is a critical disservice to reading the story as a valorization of a work ethic; in everything from the actual meaning of his name to his darkly funny death, Magarac's narrative has conflicted meanings. The subversive import of the tale is endlessly useful, and though Magarac was appropriated (for example) in a series of promotional comic books released by US Steel in the 1950s, he's been symbolic of radical causes from workers' rights to immigrant activism as well. Such was Magarac's role in the 1948 children's novel,

Joe Magarac and His USA Citizen Papers by the local radical author Irwin Shapiro.

Shapiro was both a veteran of the New Deal's Federal Art Project, as well as someone who had connections to the US Communist Party (being ultimately called before the House Un-American Activities Committee to testify). Shapiro knew his congressional surroundings well, for in *Joe Magarac and His USA Citizen Papers* the cooled ingot of steel into which he'd been reincarnated was used as a curved beam in the dome of the Capitol Building. When (as a beam) he overhears two nativist senators complaining about immigrants, he melts down out of his metal form, reconstitutes as a giant man, and proceeds to destroy Washington, DC. "You bring whole U.S.A. Army to stop Joe Magarac," Shapiro writes, "But you can't do that. How you gone shoot steel man? It not hurt me one bit."

The Vanka Murals

Visible above the short skyline of the appropriately named former mill town of Millvale are the squat, yellow-bricked double spires of the St. Nicholas Croatian Church, which once competed for prominence alongside the iron manufacturers and steel mills. From the outside, St. Nicholas is indistinguishable from other ethnic churches across the western Pennsylvania landscape, but the interior presents what are the most striking set of liturgical murals of the last century, painted by the Croatian artist Maksimilijan "Max" Vanka. Twenty-five of them produced between 1937 and 1941, Vanka's style has variously evoked the social realism of the Works Progress Administration, the communist allegories of his Mexican contemporary Diego Rivera, and the iconography of his native Croatia. Vanka's are the sort of tableaux that are surprising to see in a church, seemingly owing as much to Karl Marx as they do scripture. The artist's genius is in demonstrating how such a synthesis is anything but contradictory. "These murals are my contribution to America," Vanka said to the congregation while in the midst of painting them.

Art historian Barbara McCloskey writes in "The Millvale Murals of Maxo Vanka: Background and Analysis" that the artist's work "demonstrate his profound knowledge of Byzantine church decoration and Croatian folk art. Integrating such traditional elements into an otherwise thoroughly modern artistic vocabulary derived from Mexican muralism, turn-of-the-century European symbolism, and the most recent developments in surrealism." McCloskey claims that Vanka's work represents "an important and as yet understudied example of eastern European modernism." Vanka's murals bear titles like *The Capitalist,* an image of a vampiric, gaunt, ashen-faced, dead-eyed industrialist in top hat and frock coat, sneering with thin lip while reading stock reports behind a massive feast. For the proletarian parishioners of St. Nicholas, working in the mills of Frick and Carnegie, living in homes owned by the Mellons, passing institutions named for Westinghouse and Heinz, *The Capitalist* would have cut a familiar figure.

As if to visually embody the dialectic between labor and capital, directly opposite from *The Capitalist* is *Croatian Family,* a depiction of men in overalls and women in babushkas eating from a loaf of bread; the dark, Satanic mills of the Allegheny River Valley in the foreground while Christ ethereally floats behind the shoulder of the father, offering a benediction to the sacrament of this simple supper, as if to signal where his sympathies lay in the conflict between management and workers. Journalist Louis Adamic, writing for *Time* magazine while Vanka was working on his compositions, noted that "It was well toward the end of May before the final murals complementing these on the back walls took shape and made the women on their way out after mass stop and weep and burn candles." It seems the congregants made their sympathies clear as well.

An even more radical work is *Battlefield,* where a purple-robed Virgin Mary with a tortured face snaps the rifles of two Great War doughboys who'd been lunging at one another, a cloud of shrapnel and debris rising up and visible through the transparency of her halo. Near the choir is Vanka's depiction of the Crucifixion, the striking, pained greenish face of the son of God equal parts medieval icon and surrealist nightmare, the centurion who pierced Christ's side now a soldier with a bayonet. Across from the church's pieta there is *The Immigrant Mother Raises Her Sons for Industry,* with a veiled Croatian woman who looks nothing so much like the Virgin Mary herself, crying in front of the taut, muscular body of her son who was killed in a mill accident; men trudging to work in the background—for not even death can still labor.

Presiding hauntingly over the fallen carnage of industry and militarism is the spirit of injustice, a tall, black-robed, almost avian creature in a gas mask, holding a bloody sword above the scene. Art historians can explain how medieval cathedrals translated theology and biblical narrative into a universal, vernacular code of images; in Millvale, Vanka's murals provide a similar service, enacting a salient condemnation of injustice while producing some of the most haunting and powerful anti-capitalist, anti-imperialist, and anti-militaristic art composed in the last hundred years.

McCloskey extols "Vanka's sympathy for the exploited, the downtrodden, and the disenfranchised," imagining that his "Millvale murals preserve an awareness of the conflicts and possibilities that defined Pittsburgh, its social fabric, and its role in what America was and the promise of what it could be in the modern era." Only some four miles from the gleaming glass towers of downtown Pittsburgh, the headquarters of US Steel, BNY-Mellon, PNC Bank, and PPG are visible from the cupola of St. Nicholas, and the interior of the church is illustrated with the half-remembered sketches of heaven and hell, a manifesto against capitalism rendered in the visions of a prophet.

Billy Strayhorn Meets Duke Ellington

When the prodigy Billy Strayhorn first met Duke Ellington on a December evening in 1938, introduced to the band leader in the latter's dressing room backstage at the Stanley Theater, he was only twenty-three. Fifteen years the junior of Ellington, who was already dubbed the "King of Jazz" by the national Black newspaper the *Pittsburgh Courier,* Strayhorn was a slight, skinny, bookish, effeminate man who paid his bills by working at a Point Breeze pharmacy as a soda jerk. A circuitous work connection is what allowed Strayhorn to meet Ellington, who was used to the admiration of young fans. Strayhorn already had a reputation as a talent in Pittsburgh's jazz scene, having written a sophisticated classical composition that was played at his graduation from Westinghouse High School five years before—he'd since gone on to compose and arrange for a local jazz ensemble with the name of the Mad Hatters.

Now in downtown Pittsburgh, only a few miles from clubs like the Sawdust Trail and the Crawford Grill (sponsor of the Negro League baseball team that bore their name) that lined Wylie and Centre Avenues in the Hill, and which earned that neighborhood the sobriquet "the Crossroads of the World" by the Harlem Renaissance poet Claude McKay, Strayhorn would formally meet the most famous American composer. Strayhorn confidently sat at the piano, and with perfect verisimilitude was able to imitate Ellington's songs like "In a Sentimental Mood" and "Caravan," *and to then demonstrate the ways in which their arrangements could be improved.* Then the twenty-three-year-old soda jerk performed some of his own compositions. Ellington, immediately recognizing Strayhorn's genius, and true to the democratic ethos of jazz itself, invited the younger man to New York so they could collaborate. Strayhorn jotted down Ellington's directions uptown, with the line "Take the A Train" becoming the title of his most famous song, and the theme of the orchestra itself.

The two would forge the most productive creative partnership of the twentieth century. Strayhorn would compose and arrange standards for Ellington's orchestra, including "Satin Doll" and "Lush Life." Despite Strayhorn's relative anonymity, Ellington always acknowledged the talent and genius of those contributions. David Hajdu writes in *Lush Life: A Biography of Billy Strayhorn* that the musician, who wrote "hit songs, jazz pieces, concert works, film scores, music for a Broadway show," was often viewed as "Ellington's alter ego" who "wrote in a style so akin to Ellington's that few people could distinguish their work." Debates have long raged between those who view Strayhorn as fundamentally a rustic who was tutored by Ellington, and those who see him as the musical power behind the throne. "Promulgated for years," Hajdu writes of both sides, and "none of this turned out to be so simple." As an arranger, Strayhorn was unparalleled, and Ellington would declare that he was "my right arm, my left arm, all the eyes in the back of my head, my brain waves in his head, and his in mine." To reduce either man's contributions is to fundamentally misunderstand jazz and the nature of collaboration, what critic Ted Gioia describes in *The History of Jazz* as being the case where Strayhorn "became a true partner, playing a pivotal role in shaping the band's sound."

Strayhorn was urbane, elegant, sophisticated, and openly homosexual; the lyricist who in "Lush Life" could write that "I used to visit all the very gay places / Those come what may places / Where one relaxes on the axis of the wheel of life / To get the feel of life… / From jazz and cocktails." Though classical music was his first love, it was an impossibility that a Black man of his generation could build a career in that elitist realm, but he brought a symphonic sensibility to his collaborations, including Ellington's *Black, Brown and Beige,* which premiered in 1943 at New York's Carnegie Hall. Despite a cosmopolitan life in New York and Paris, it was the Black community in Pittsburgh that birthed Strayhorn: the Homewood where he was educated (once answering that all of his genius was learned in high school) and the Hill District where he first became conversant with jazz.

When Pittsburgh's neighborhoods were filling with immigrants from places like Vilnius, Krakow, and Naples, there were also thousands of Black Americans arriving from the areas around Birmingham, Atlanta, and Greensboro (Strayhorn's maternal family was from North Carolina) as part of the Great Migration, the single-largest internal movement in American history. Journalist Mark Whitaker notes in *Smoketown: The Untold Story of the Other Great Black Renaissance* that the community these migrants built in the Hill District was "for a brief but glorious stretch of the twentieth century, one of the most vibrant and consequential communities of color in U.S. history." Central to Black life in Pittsburgh was jazz, and as the city was almost equidistant from New York and Chicago, it became a regular part of the circuit of musicians who performed in its clubs night after night.

The Hill's clubs were not just a stage for visiting musicians, but for the city's own performers, with Whitaker celebrating this "black version of the story of fifteenth-century Florence and early-twentieth-century Vienna: a miraculous flowering of social and cultural achievement all at once, in one small city." Over the next few decades, Hill District clubs would be the university for a cadre of Pittsburgh jazz performers, including not just Strayhorn, but singer Billy Eckstine, pianist Erroll Garner, pianist Mary Lou Williams, drummer Art Blakey, trumpeter Roy Eldridge, pianist Ahmad Jamal, drummer

Kenny Clarke, bassist Paul Chambers, bassist Ray Brown, and the great platonic love of Strayhorn's life, the singer and actress Lena Horne, who claimed that had the composer not been gay, she would have surely married him.

What resulted was America's greatest cultural contribution: our own indigenous music. In the canonized realm of those who contributed to that mission, Strayhorn is an invaluable member of the pantheon. Conventional wisdom has configured Strayhorn as dwelling in Ellington's shadow, but that's an incomplete understanding of his significance. The two were halves of a greater talent, they were twined aspects of the same personality, the same inspiration, the same genius. And the songs—the melancholic pining of "Lush Life," the sultry eroticism of "Satin Doll," the sheer, joyful expression of "Take the A Train," a composition that said so much about American modernity.

"I'll live a lush life in some small dive," wrote Strayhorn, "And there I'll be / While I rot with the rest / of those whose lives are lonely too." It was esophageal cancer that would take him in 1967, exacerbated by years of alcoholism, the only thing that he'd inherited from his father. Two years later and Ellington would release an album in his partner's honor entitled . . . *And His Mother Called Him Bill*. The last track was recorded by accident, Ellington performing Strayhorn's composition "Lotus Blossom" unaccompanied on piano while the rest of the band members packed up their instruments and left the studio.

Horseshoe Curve

On June 12, 1942, the Nazi German submarine U-202 made ground some hundred miles to the east of New York City on a stretch of beach on the south side of Long Island. Manned by eight German sailors, the crew of George Dasch, Ernst Burger, Herbert Haupt, Edward Kerling, Richard Quirin, Heinrich Heinck, Herman Neubauer, and Werner Thiel had in their possession schematics of several facilities around the country. The purpose of "Operation Pastorius" was to sabotage key military and industrial sites that would hamper America's waging of the Second World War. Ironically named after the prominent seventeenth-century German Pennsylvanian immigrant and mystic Daniel Pastorius, who was a committed pacifist, the purpose of the mission was not just to cripple American military power, but to spread terror as well.

Four days later, a second group of Abwehr agents disembarked from the submarine U-584 on a beach near Jacksonville, Florida. Both missions were able to successfully penetrate the nation's defenses, with the first landing party simply taking Long Island Rail into Manhattan, and the second traveling by train to Chicago. Both groups were to meet on Independence Day in Cincinnati to begin the second portion of their operations, but the day before the landing in Jacksonville, Dasch called the FBI to inform on his coconspirators. Dasch confessed that it was the Abwehr's intent, by direct orders from Adolph Hitler, to destroy several installations, including New York City bridges, a train station in New Jersey, hydroelectric plants on the Niagara River, locks in Kentucky, midwestern and Southern plants of the Aluminum Company of America, and, most crucially, a stretch of railroad a little under a hundred miles east of Pittsburgh in Altoona, Pennsylvania, known by the name of "Horseshoe Curve."

Michael Dobbs explains, in *Saboteurs: The Nazi Raid on America*, the strategic importance of Horseshoe Curve, a 2,375-foot stretch of railway constructed in 1854 that looped through an Allegheny mountain pass overlooking a steep incline into a man-made reservoir. Dobbs writes that the Nazis understood the curve to be among the nation's "critical bottlenecks." For almost a century, the tracks going through Horseshoe Curve were the quickest and most efficient way to move passengers and products across the mountainous spine of Pennsylvania, connecting the Commonwealth's two distant metropolises. During World War II, this became more than just an issue of convenience, as Pittsburgh once again configured itself as the "Arsenal of Democracy." Joseph F. Rishel writes in his collected oral histories, *Pittsburgh Remembers World War II*, that the "changing economy and the ever-decreasing male workforce opened up opportunities that were not available prior to the war," when necessity compelled steel mills to open employment for women. From those mills came the staggering ninety-five million tons of steel that would prove necessary.

From the Edgar Thompson Works and the Homestead Works came the raw material that was being pressed into use for the sands of North Africa, the atolls of the South Pacific, the beaches of Normandy. Rishel explains that the year the Operation Pastorius agents were arrested, "90,000 Americans were forced to surrender to the Japanese in the Philippines, Japan proceeded to take over much of the East Asia and the western Pacific . . . the Germans were deep into Russia. In Africa, they were . . . within striking distance of Great Britain's oil lifeline, the Suez Canal." While it's often been rightly said that Great Britain, and especially the Soviet Union, suffered the brunt of human casualties in the actual war, Pittsburgh manufacturing played the central "role in reversing the dismal world picture," as Rishel writes.

Royal Air Force planes sent to Britain under the provisions of President Franklin Roosevelt's Lend-Lease program were made of steel forged in Homestead, just as the vehicles landing at Omaha and Utah Beach were made of iron forged alongside the Monongahela. Joseph Stalin told Roosevelt at Tehran that the war had been won with "British intelligence . . . Russian blood, [and American steel]." If the United States would see itself propelled into the status of a superpower after the end of the war, then so too would its greatest industrial city see itself at the height of its economic and political power.

By the end of the war, Pittsburgh's population would be the highest in its history, near 680,000 people, making it the tenth largest city in the country—the last time it would ever be that large.

The Frank Lloyd Wright Plan

With a deserved reputation for an obstinacy comparable to his brilliance, the celebrated architect Frank Lloyd Wright supposedly told a gathering of Carnegie Tech engineering students in 1949 that "Pittsburgh is interesting, you might say, but so is a collision between a truck, a school bus and five cars. The boys who made their money here ran away and left you to live in this pile of scrap." Fourteen years before, and as a guest of the department store magnate Edgar Kaufmann, Wright told reporters that rather than suggesting alterations that could be made to the architectural landscape, "It would be cheaper to abandon it and build a real one. This is a disappearing city: nothing comes out of it. The ancients would have swooned at the mere mention of the money it cost to build this jumble of buildings."

Wright protested too loudly, for the unmistakable drama of the landscape—valleys and mountains cut through with wide rivers—was irresistible to his own sense of grandeur. As Wright had designed Fallingwater, the Kaufmann's summer home in the Laurel Highlands some seventy miles east of the city, with its audacious waterfall running through the living room, so too did he dream of imprinting his vision on the three rivers. Two years before he dismissed the terrain as the aesthetic equivalent of a car pileup, Wright had been invited by Kaufmann to submit designs for the urban redevelopment of the Point, at the time a collection of derelict warehouses, abandoned factories, and unsightly bridges.

Wright produced two different designs for Pittsburgh's civic leaders, both for the construction of a Point Park Civic

Center. The first was a massive structure containing theaters, a stadium, an opera hall, and a convention center; the second was a sleek modernist ziggurat connecting itself by pedestrian bridges across the rivers. Adjusted for inflation, Wright's project would cost a minimum of five billion dollars. Never one to internalize accurate appraisals of his character, Wright would dismiss his rejection by the Allegheny Conference on Community Development by asking, "Is it impractical to spend several hundred million to further your culture?"

Urban designer Michael Benedikt notes in *God, Creativity, and Evolution: The Argument from Designers* that "Wright thought not that he was God but that he brought or allowed God into the world through what he did, creating and designing." The committee was composed of practical men, even if no less idealistic than Wright in their own way. This was the committee that took as its mission "an exploration of . . . Pittsburgh's possible future . . . prepared on the premise that there will be an expansion in the civilized use of intellect, heart, science, and technology." Wright's hubris may have prevented him from understanding that the committee held to its own singular vision as well, and the quixotic plans of an avant-garde architect wouldn't stall their aspirations for urban renewal. The architect may have had his God, and more importantly his patron in Kaufmann, but he had neither Mayor David L. Lawrence nor banker Richard King Mellon, who together dominated the Allegheny Conference.

Lawrence, a product of Pittsburgh's Irish slums and ultimately the first Catholic to be elected to the governor's mansion, was a stolid Democrat, leading what had been until the New Deal a thoroughly Republican city (like most northern metropolises). Mellon was a well-heeled conservative, a pro-business Republican, a prince in the city's WASP aristocracy, and a scion of the most powerful family in the United States. Both were conversant in the language of politics, albeit not just from different ideological positions but from an entirely separate rhetoric of experience as well. Mellon was the nephew of Andrew Mellon, Herbert Hoover's secretary of the Treasury, and the founder of the National Gallery of Art. Unlike Mellon, Lawrence's political instincts were not inherited, but rather earned. The mayor started his political career as chairman of the Allegheny Democratic Party, later running local offices on behalf of New York governor Al Smith's 1928 presidential campaign.

By the time Lawrence was elected in 1946, he'd helped to build a powerful Irish Catholic Democratic political machine, which despite (or perhaps because of) its politics of backroom, smoky dealings was vociferously progressive. Historian Michael Weber writes in *Don't Call Me Boss: David L. Lawrence, Pittsburgh's Renaissance Mayor* that "he proved to be a man with a broader vision and an innate sense of the operation of government and politics." It was Lawrence's switching of Pennsylvania's delegates to Franklin Roosevelt at the 1932 Democratic National Convention that helped ensure the governor's election. As political boss in 1948, he delivered Pittsburgh's votes to Harry Truman when he was unpopular in the wider party, and by 1960, Lawrence's hold on Pennsylvania Democratic politics was so complete that John F. Kennedy felt he had no choice but to agree to the Pittsburgher's demand that Lyndon Johnson be added to the ticket. With four men making it to the White House because of his endorsements and strategizing, Lawrence's reputation as "president maker" was well-earned. Against a personality like that, what hope did Wright have?

Despite their ideological and partisan differences, both Lawrence and Mellon were stalwart advocates of what would be understood today as environmentalism, and both shared a common drive to completely redesign the gritty, decayed, rusting core of Pittsburgh. With Lawrence providing the political will and Mellon the financial capabilities, the two initiated the first phase of what would be called "Renaissance I." Despite the ultimate lack of Wright's Ozymandian pyramids, Renaissance I would, for both good and bad, demolish and rebuild vast blocks of the city. Over three decades after the founding of the Allegheny Committee, their vision would be enacted in projects like Point State Park (in lieu of Wright's design), and the construction of a gleaming new skyline with corporate headquarters for US Steel, Westinghouse, Pittsburgh Plate Glass, and Mellon Bank (among others). Perhaps most crucially, the two men were also the driving force behind the adoption of new air quality ordinances.

Writing in *Imagining the Modern: Architecture and Urbanism of the Pittsburgh Renaissance,* Rami el Samahy and Chris Grimley describe the "ambitious program of revitalization . . . [that] transformed Pittsburgh and quickly became a model for other U.S. cities." There would be hideous oversights as well, as "renewal" would destroy neighborhoods from the Hill District to East Liberty (both largely Black), and the worst excesses of Robert Moses inspired constructions threatened the historical integrity of the landscape. Yet Grimley and el Samahy still argue that Pittsburgh's Renaissance is best understood, contra Wright's denunciations, as a crucial example of American aesthetic modernism, when "Pittsburgh was at the center of the world stage." Even Wright was able to get something out of the renewal, if not the actual commission. He recycled his designs, as always attracted to the curving lines and circles that he'd once imagined rising up over the Allegheny, Monongahela, and Ohio, appropriating them rather to rise above New York's Fifth Avenue, where they'd be incorporated into a museum known as the Guggenheim.

A Gladstone High School Dropout

August Wilson could read entire books by the time he was four. A survival skill, allowing him to forge a private utopia of words, composing his own autodidact's syllabus of Ralph Ellison, James Baldwin, and Langston Hughes, whom he discovered amongst the stacks of the main branch of the Carnegie Library while he was still only in elementary school. This paradise of text was instrumental in Wilson's sense of self, sense of identity, sense of endurance. Born to a German baker, who'd immigrated from the Sudetenland, and a Black domestic worker, who'd moved to Pittsburgh from North Carolina, the Hill District would be the site of Wilson's formative years, and forever the imagined country to which the writer would return.

When he was only five, he and his mother moved to the working-class Hungarian neighborhood of Hazelwood, where youths threw bricks through the family windows and racial invective was daily directed at them. Wilson kicked around several different high schools—Central Catholic, Connelly Vocational—until dropping out of Gladstone in 1960. He'd written a twenty-page essay about Napoleon, for which his teacher had accused him of plagiarism. Embarrassed, enraged, and ashamed, Wilson received nothing more in the way of official, credentialed education, though he'd go on to indisputably become one of the greatest American dramatists.

Years later, after he'd won Pulitzers and the Heinz Award, the Carnegie Library would grant him an honorary high school diploma, something more honorable to him than an honorary doctorate. Wilson's entire oeuvre was an acknowledgement that there is as much wisdom among sanitation workers as in a seminar, as much knowledge in a pool hall as at a symposium. In conversation with the *Paris Review,* Wilson noted of the characters in his plays that audiences were forced to see people like a "garbageman, a person they don't really look at, although they see a garbageman every day." Consequently, his mostly white audiences watching a mostly Black cast will "find out that the content of this black garbageman's life is affected by the same things—love, honor, beauty, betrayal, duty."

Such are the universal themes Wilson explored in his unprecedented ten plays, one for each decade of the twentieth century, which constitute *The Pittsburgh Cycle.* More than twenty hours of stage time, plays like *Jitney, Joe Turner's Come and Gone, The Piano Lesson, Seven Guitars, King Hedley II,* and his most celebrated work, *Fences.* Then there are his characters, enormous and flawed women and men, from Jim Becker, who manages a station for unlicensed cabs (called jitneys, hence the name of the play), to the conflicted wealthy developer and mayoral candidate Harmond Wilks in *Radio Golf,* and of course volatile Troy Maxon and his dignified wife, Rose, in *Fences.*

For a city that has produced so many novelists and poets, including Annie Dillard, John Edgar Wideman, Michael Chabon, Stewart O'Nan, Jack Gilbert, W. D. Snodgrass, and Gerald Stern, none quite did what Wilson accomplished. Harkening back to the cycles of the great Athenian playwrights, Wilson's *Pittsburgh Cycle* explored in exacting detail the particulars of a Black neighborhood across the long sweep of the century. Like Sophocles, Wilson examines the capricious punishments of the fates, but in his case, the structural inequities of America are the true furies. As his character Aunt Ester Tyler, who claims to be a 285-year-old "soul cleanser," says in the earliest play of his cycle, *Gem of the Ocean* (although the penultimate to be written, all of the plays having been composed out of order): "See that right there . . .

that's a city. It's only a half mile by a half mile but that's a city. It's made of bones. Pearly white bones. All the buildings and everything is made of bones."

Wilson learned dialogue from Wylie Avenue bars and Black Power meetings, from working in kitchens and from Black Arts Movements poetry workshops on Centre Avenue. Critic Patrick Maley argues in *After August: Blues, August Wilson, and American Drama* that Wilson created "blues dramaturgy," for in the tradition of the blues, he "found not simply a musical genre, but rather a performative mode of joining with community in a shared project of understanding the self and others vis-à-vis history, ancestry, art, spirituality, politics, pain, and joy." This was the consummate rhetoric of barstool and front stoop bullshit artistry, the poetry of Troy in *Fences* saying, "Death ain't nothing. I done seen him. Done wrassled with him. You can't tell me nothing about death. Death ain't nothing but a fastball on the outside corner."

The Pittsburgh Cycle is ambivalent about its subject, even while the grid of Pittsburgh's streets and alleys were superimposed onto his consciousness. Scholar Sandra G. Shannon writes in the introduction to her anthology *August Wilson's Pittsburgh Cycle: Critical Perspectives on the Plays* that "writing these plays . . . connected his angst with that of the larger African-American community." Wilson's Pittsburgh indelibly shaped him, but he was not Pollyannaish about the city or its persistent racism. *The Pittsburgh Cycle* is a love letter not to Pittsburgh, but to its Black community shut out of lucrative jobs in the mills, segregated from the main life of the community. As he told journalist Bill Moyers, the "real struggle has been since Africans first set foot on the continent, an affirmation of the value of one's self." *The Pittsburgh Cycle* is an affirmation, a compendium of dreams and nightmares, shouts and cries, lullabies, fairy tales, protests, denunciations, petitions, manifestos, theorizing, and the dozens.

Perhaps that's what Troy means when he says, "Death ain't nothing to play with. And I know he's gonna get me . . . But as long as I keep my strength and see him coming . . . he's gonna have to fight to get me. I ain't going easy."

World Series Champions

Underneath the shadow of the Cathedral of Learning, dyed black from the smog that had only recently been cleaned from Pittsburgh's atmosphere, New York Yankee pitcher Ralph Terry faced off against Pirates' batter Bill Mazeroski within the brick temple that was Forbes Field. Bottom of the ninth with bases loaded, the greatly favored Yankees were tied with the Bucs 9-9 when the Maz hit a home run sending the ball out over left field, past Yogi Berra's glove, over the red brick and green ivy of the stadium's wall, and seemingly beyond the Carnegie and the Cathedral and into the fabled halls of Cooperstown.

When he was asked how he felt following the game, the Maz said, "Only joy and celebration." When Berra was asked what had gone wrong for the boys in pinstripes, the catcher responded, "We made too many wrong mistakes." It was the Pirates' first championship since 1925, with the final inning of the 1960 World Series remaining the only one clinched in game seven by a single home run.

Scholar of Renaissance literature, Yale University president, commissioner of Major League Baseball, and unfortunate Boston Red Sox fan A. Bartlett Giamatti wrote that "there is a rough justice" to the game, a reminder from "Dame Mutability" to the "Yankees of how slight and fragile are the circumstances that exalt one group of human beings over another." For Pittsburghers, there is not just poetry in sports but liturgy as well. In the genuflections of Pittsburgh sports, the stations of the cross that go through recounted victories and defeats, the Maz's winning home run occupies a special resonance, for it signifies a sense of how even when tied at the bottom of the ninth in the seventh game, there is the possibility for the laws of the cosmos to seemingly suspend and for the good guys to win—at least for a time.

The Yankees roster included names like Berra, Turley, and Mickey Mantle (who admitted later to having wept in the locker room), while the upstart Pirates featured Mazeroski and a young outfielder born in Puerto Rico who was playing his fifth season named Roberto Clemente. John McCollister and Ralph Kiner described the hero of game seven in *The Bucs!: The Story of the Pittsburgh Pirates* as being the "tobacco-chewing Ohio coal miner's son Bill Mazeroski." The team's victory in the 1960 World Series signaled the second coming for the Pirates, a renewal of the promise exemplified by players like Honus Wagner from decades before, who'd been a shortstop when the sport itself was still young, while looking forward to the Bucs' glorious ascendancy when Clemente took them to victory in 1971. In a game that proves the patience of Americans who are so often libeled as being allergic to that virtue, there are certain pivotal moments within its history that are remembered as almost transcendent.

Mazeroski worked a miracle, but Pittsburgh's Christ was the right fielder Clemente. Black and Hispanic in a segregated city, the now celebrated Clemente was horribly mistreated by both fans and local media, mocked for his accent and dismissed because of his race. Yet his leadership would prove instrumental in the Pirates' 1971 World Series win, and he'd be remembered as one of the most talented athletes to play the game, as well as one of its most quietly charismatic personalities. David Maraniss writes in *Clemente: The Passion and Grace of Baseball's Last Hero* that "Clemente was not the greatest who ever played the game . . . yet there was something about him that elevated him into his own realm."

Comporting himself with an understated dignity, Clemente used his position, power, influence, and wealth to pursue philanthropic relief missions, assisting women and men in communities much like the one in which he grew up. "The mythic aspects of baseball usually draw on clichés of the innocent past, the nostalgia for how things were," writes Maraniss. "But Clemente's myth arcs the other way, to the future . . . to what people hope they can become." Following an earthquake in Nicaragua less than a year after his last World Series win, Clemente accompanied a plane filled with food and medicine. The right-wing junta of dictator Anastasio Somoza Debayle had been diverting previous flights, and Clemente believed that his presence would ensure its safe arrival. Overloaded by almost 4,200 pounds, the plane crashed near Clemente's home of Puerto Rico, his body never to be recovered.

Coca-Cola and Marilyn Monroe

Eleanor Ward's Stable Gallery on Manhattan's Upper East Side had been influential in promoting the abstract expressionists who dominated the American art scene after the Second World War; men like Jackson Pollock and Willem de Kooning who practiced a brash, expressive, nonrepresentational type of composition. What made the abstract expressionists so radical is that they refused to depict anything, but Ward had already ensured that it would soon be passé. On November 6, 1962, she would have an opening at her East Seventy-Fourth Street gallery for a new type of art and a new type of artist. Rather than depicting nothing, this new artist chose to represent the most mundane of objects: Coke cans, Campbell's Soup cans, and Marilyn Monroe's face. The artist's name was Andy Warhol, he was from South Oakland, and he'd become the most important artist of the century.

His image is instantly recognizable—the lanky, pale, androgynous man with the platinum white wig. So identified is he with New York City, where he produced the Velvet Underground in the 1960s and mentored '80s enfants terribles like Jean-Michel Basquiat and Keith Haring (whose first art show had been in Mellon Park's Pittsburgh Center for the Arts), that it can seem incongruous to imagine Warhol as coming from the crooked, narrow streets of Oakland. He was the child of Lemka immigrants and the son of a coal miner; his mother and father observant adherents of the Ruthenian rite of the Catholic Church. The family would walk to Mass at St. John Chrysostom Church in Nine Mile Run every Sunday.

The openly gay Warhol left Pittsburgh in 1949 after getting a degree in commercial art from Carnegie Tech, chafing at its provincialism. Warhol's relationship to Pittsburgh was complicated; in some instances, he claimed to be from McKeesport (distinctly less glamorous), and in *The Philosophy of Andy Warhol (from A to B and Back Again)*, he succinctly said, "I come from nowhere." Biographer Wayne Koestenbaum writes in *Andy Warhol* that Pittsburgh was "a city he did not pick," that it was a "despised zone of his past—city of steel, whose color is silver." Warhol would rather become symbolic of New York grit at the height of its elegant danger; he was not of the Monongahela, but of Mick Jagger and Lou Reed; he was not of the Allegheny, but of Blondie and the Exploding Plastic Inevitable.

Warhol's studio was first on the Lower East Side, then Union Square, and finally on Broadway, which he christened with the most Pittsburgh name possible—the Factory. There, true to his Pittsburgh roots, Warhol found a way to mechanize the avant-garde, and to turn painting into commodity. "What's great about this country," he either ironically or unironically (it was hard to tell) gushed in *The Philosophy of Andy Warhol,* was that "America started the tradition where the richest consumers buy essentially the same things as the poorest. You can be watching TV and see Coca-Cola, and know the President drinks Coca-Cola, Liz Taylor drinks Coca-Cola, and just think you can drink Coca-Cola too."

Two years after the show at the Stable Gallery, art critic Arthur Danto would note of one of Warhol's more infamous sculptures: "What in the end makes the difference between a Brillo box and a work of art consisting of a Brillo box is a certain theory of art . . . that takes it up into the world of art, and keeps it from collapsing into the real object which it is." Warhol doesn't collapse the distinction between art and life, but rather elevates the latter into the former, even while Danto notes that such "could not have been art fifty years ago." Warhol's dedication to the things of this world was in one sense incredibly Catholic in its immanence, and in another incredibly democratic.

With an immigrant's love of capitalism, the things Warhol celebrated in his art were the same unpretentious things that his Oakland neighbors would have consumed—Coke, Campbell's Soup, celebrity pinups. Something intrinsically Pittsburgh came from the Factory's assembly line. Warhol's colorful celebrity portraits looked nothing so much like the icons of his youth. He moved his beloved mother Julia from Pittsburgh to his Manhattan apartment, attending Mass every day at St. Vincent Ferrer, where he only crossed himself in the manner of the Byzantine Rite and never took the Eucharist.

When he died of kidney failure in 1987, Warhol's confidant and the editor of *Interview* magazine, Bob Colacello, remembers in *Holy Terror: Andy Warhol Close Up* that "one hundred mourners assembled in the onion-domed Holy Ghost Byzantine Rite Catholic Church on Pittsburgh's working-class North Side," near where, in a decade, a museum would be dedicated to him. Following the funeral, both the working-class Pittsburghers and the beautiful people from the Factory "went to the $7.95-per-head-chicken-and-dumpling lunch arranged by Andy's sister-in-law Margaret Warhola at a nearby restaurant called the Mona Lisa Lounge." He would be buried in Bethel Park, his coffin containing a copy of *Interview* and a bottle of Estée Lauder perfume, with the grave marked by a set of rosaries and a Campbell's Soup can.

The Hill District Riots

Tanks rolled up Centre Avenue and over 3,000 Pennsylvania National Guardsman marched into Pittsburgh on April 5, 1968, while the Hill District burnt for several nights following Martin Luther King's assassination. Hundreds of businesses were destroyed, a thousand arrests were made, and at least one person died. Entire swaths of the North Side, Homewood, and the Hill District were immolated, with blocks left over to entropy. Such an explosion wasn't unique to Pittsburgh; similar or worse riots decimated Washington, Baltimore, and Detroit, though the civil unrest in the Hill would finalize the destruction that began two decades earlier with urban renewal projects that cratered out the district.

While institutionalized Jim Crow may have been technically illegal north of the Mason-Dixon Line, Pittsburgh was like other northern cities in high levels of segregation and wealth disparity between its citizens. Following King's assassination, there was an explosion of rage in those cities, where the rioting said as much about the daily injustices that defined Black life as it did the event that triggered the reaction. Following the riots, Brandeis University public policy professor Ralph W. Conant would testify before a task force on the immediate causes of the violence. "What white Pittsburgh must understand," said Conant, "is that black Pittsburgh had to riot before a sense of urgency about ghetto problems was generated in the white community."

Conant's point was crucial, for Pittsburgh was (and is), in many ways, two communities rather than one. In 1961, the Hill was cut off from downtown Pittsburgh, less than a mile to the west, with the construction of the massive domed Civic Arena, promoted by Kaufmann and endorsed by the Allegheny Conference. Partially inspired by the similar brutalist aesthetics of New York urban planner Robert Moses, the Civic Arena was a master class in massive works designed to impress, with little regard for their function. Urban theorist Jane Jacobs despaired about these sorts of projects, writing in *The Death and Life of Great American Cities* that "we have become so feckless as a people that we no longer care how things do work, but only what kind of quick, easy outer impression they give." Replaced was the dynamic community of the Hill, in favor of the steel boil that was the Civic Arena.

Initially conceived of as a home for the Civic Light Opera, and featuring the world's largest retractable roof, the Civic Arena would ultimately house the Pittsburgh Penguins hockey team, who would play (and lose) their first game to the Montreal Canadians a year before the riots. Toker explains that other sites had been considered, including Oakland, Squirrel Hill, and Highland Park, but that the "Hill had no powerful civic voice to offer protest, so it was selected for the construction scheme." Development on the arena began in 1955 and would see the seizure of over 400 Black-owned businesses through eminent domain, and the relocation of 8,000 residents of the Hill District to neighborhoods like East Liberty and Homewood.

If the riots were both in reaction to an incredibly local situation and a national injustice, then the city similarly convulsed around other issues as well. Pennsylvania would become home to more than a quarter of a million Vietnam veterans, and close to a thousand Pittsburghers would die in Southeast Asia. So connected is the region to the image of the blue-collar worker uncomplicatedly fighting when their draft number is pulled, that the vibrant and massive anti-war movement is too often eclipsed. Far less attention is paid to the radical organizing among the working class for civil and labor rights and against the war. Historian Jefferson R. Cowie describes in *Stayin' Alive: The 1970s and the Last Days of the Working Class* how in 1968, the University of Pittsburgh was visited by Joseph Yablonski, president of the United Mine Workers, who "invited students to join not just in the working people's fight against wealth and privilege but also the struggle 'to get the hell out of Vietnam!' at a moment when organized labor was one of the most aggressive defenders of U.S. foreign policy."

Pittsburgh, like the country at large, found itself at a cultural impasse as the 1960s turned into the '70s. Strung between the machinations of the Democratic machine politicians and the utopianism of the New Left, split between Black and white, the Protestant aristocracy and the second-generation immigrant working class. In some sense, the city found itself as prominent, powerful, and secure as it would ever be, still a symbol of the consequence of America. But privatization and deregulation threatened the security that was represented by the idea of a solid job, even if the example of neighborhoods razed in the interests of civic "progress" belied how contingent that dream was.

The Immaculate Reception

Steelers' owner Art Rooney was actually walking back to his office when it happened, assuming that they would never be able to pull it out with only thirty seconds left and Pittsburgh trailing the Raiders 7-6. That was when Terry Bradshaw attempted to throw a pass to John "Frenchy" Fuqua, who dropped the ball when tackled, only to have fullback Franco Harris appear seemingly from nowhere, rescue the ball from extinction on the ground of Three Rivers Stadium, and score a touchdown. Myron Cope, the waggish sportscaster and the gloriously accented "Voice of the Steelers" for WTAE-FM radio, called the play the "Immaculate Reception," and the name for Franco's miraculous save stuck. A fusion of the sacred and the profane, for as Jason Zemcik notes in *Black and Gold Dynasty: The Championship History of the Pittsburgh Steelers,* this is a city where it's expected that churches will change "mass times on Sundays in January because missing kickoff for a playoff game would be its own form of sacrilege."

The Steelers would dominate football, when in the 1970s, they'd win the Super Bowl an astounding four times with their defensive "Steel Curtain," going on into subsequent decades to be tied for the most titles ever won. The team of Bradshaw, defensive tackle "Mean" Joe Green, linebacker Jack Lambert— all of them intimidating as hell. In '72, however, they were known as lovable losers. Sportswriter Roy Blount Jr., true to his name, writes in *About Three Bricks Shy of a Load: A Highly Irregular Lowdown on the Year the Pittsburgh Steelers were Super but Missed the Bowl,* that "People—including a good many in Pittsburgh—tend to look upon Pittsburgh as a Loser town."

Blount continues by hypothesizing about the origin of this cringe: "Perhaps it is the 'Pitts' in the name. . . . Perhaps it is the immigrant millworker image. . . . Perhaps it is the fact that Pittsburgh has never been westerly enough to imply frontiersmen, easterly enough to imply sophisticates. . . . Perhaps it is the fact that the Steelers went forty years without a championship." Such was the context whereby Harris's victory could seem as a bit of divine intervention, the first time the team had ever won a playoff game. Few subjects, for better or for worse, are as intrinsically associated with Pittsburgh identity quite like football, and the Steelers are better known and more celebrated than the now defunct industry from whence they draw their name. The Steelers have served as the locus of regional identity; the no-fuss working-class, blue-collar team, overseen by the benevolent Irish Catholic patriarchs of the Rooneys who don't countenance gimmicks like cheerleaders or mascots (until recently), in favor of rough football that favors the ass-saving play in the last seconds of the fourth quarter (as exemplified by Harris's touchdown).

Zemcik writes that the "beaming sense of pride, the feeling of community that being a Pittsburgh Steelers fan brings" is related to the fact that "the mills closed and western Pennsylvanians were forced to scatter across the country in droves." For many Pittsburghers, the Steelers are a secularized faith with its own rituals and relics, where the unifying thread of the "Yinzer Nation" (after the derogatory term for working-class Pittsburghers) is devotion to football. Easy for some to condescend to this sort of faith, but it's to miss the point of religion—the binding together of disparate people. Much can be said about football; the macho posturing and the militarism, the spectacle and the violence. But to ignore the very tangible ways it can foster connection can't be dismissed.

When Harris was named MVP for Super Bowl IX, he became both the first African American player and the first

Italian American player to receive that award. Harris was a potent symbol of unity in a city that was and is divided on class and racial lines. Proud of his accomplishments, a pizzeria in East Liberty, founded "Franco's Italian Army" (Frank Sinatra would be a "Brigadier General") to celebrate Harris. Less than a decade after Pittsburgh burned, working-class white Pittsburghers would toast a Black man as one of their own. Even if such symbolism in the Yinzer Nation isn't everything, it's surely not nothing either.

Shadyside Presbyterian

Less than three blocks from where Pittsburgh's first iron furnace had once stood, a group of protestors gathered at the white-stoned gothic Shadyside Presbyterian Church in the spring and summer of 1985. Nestled on tree-lined streets next to colonial and Tudor homes, the church was among the wealthiest in the city, its pews filled with both Mellons and Heinzes, and often the leadership of United Steel. Now, the industry was in the midst of an unprecedented collapse, with Tracy Neumann explaining in *Remaking the Rust Belt: The Postindustrial Transformation of North America* that, "In the 1980s, the Pittsburgh region's shuttered plants, legions of unemployed steelworkers, and bankrupt mill towns became emblems of an emerging Rust Belt."

Neumann writes that "trade liberalization, U.S. subsidies for foreign manufacturers, and successful industrial attraction schemes in the South and the Sunbelt . . . diminished executives' commitments to the communities in which their companies were headquartered." Protesters at the church alleged in a media communique that the wealthy worshipers who owned US Steel had facilitated the "elimination of the Mon Valley steel mills, the development of small industrial parks which will hire people at wages significantly below union scale, and the development of river front condominiums and water recreation facilities for the 'new residents' of corporate Pittsburgh." By the mid-eighties the Pittsburgh region was in the midst of an almost unprecedented collapse, where unemployment levels in some towns rivaled or surpassed those of the Great Depression.

For two years US Steel and the United Steelworkers union had been at a negotiation impasse, and labor activists arrived at Shadyside Presbyterian to condemn the avarice of that industry now discarding those who'd given their lives to the corporation. It was Easter of 1984 when rebellious Rev. D. Douglas Roth and two labor activists named Mike Bonn and Darrell Becker stood in front of the Shadyside Presbyterian, with Bonn telling the press that "When a church has $7 million in the bank, has the same directors as the corporations, puts families in the street, builds a $1 million sitting room for rich ladies, it is evil against all biblical example." A year later, they returned with a pile of scrap metal, which they tried to place on the altar; all three were arrested for the protest and released later on $50,000 bond.

Reasons for this collapse are legion. Corporate defenders claim that the unions' resistance to modernization was responsible, while partisans of labor correctly surmise that it was calculated executive malpractice designed to sell the region's mills off for scrap. Part of the larger phenomenon taking place across the Midwest; the city joining Cleveland, Cincinnati, Columbus, Indianapolis, Gary, Flint, Detroit, and Milwaukee as victims of "free" trade policies based on the corporate bottom line more than workers' rights and endorsed by politicians like Ronald Reagan. Regardless of the mechanism, the process of deindustrialization was physically and socially traumatic for the region. Taking it with indomitable understatement, a worker named Ed Buzinka quoted in William Serrin's *Homestead: The Glory and Tragedy of an American Steel Town* said, "Well, that was that. . . . But I'll tell you what. It was a good run while it lasted."

Down came the kilns at Jones and Laughlin's mill on the Southside, down came the mills lining the Monongahela, down came the mighty Homestead Works itself. Labor journalist and McKeesport native John Hoerr writes of his return to western Pennsylvania in his 1988 account, *And the Wolf Finally Came: The Decline and Fall of the American Steel Industry,* describing how "As I gaze up the valley, I am struck by the absence of smoke. Not even a suggestion of a wisp hangs over the Homestead Works of U.S. Steel. . . . But something else is lacking—a sense of life, the teeming, active, energetic life the valley once knew. I dislike exaggeration, but this is what I feel: Death is in the air."

By 1983 unemployment within Allegheny Country was at 13.9 percent; the greater metropolitan region had a staggering, unadjusted number of 18.2 percent of people unemployed. According to the *Pittsburgh Post-Gazette,* the damage was far worse outside of relatively prosperous Pittsburgh. By that year, Beaver County had an unemployment rate of 27.1 percent, and in Cambria County it surpassed 23 percent. When the 1970s began, fully 300,000 people worked in Pittsburgh's steel industry, and by 1990, virtually every one of those mill jobs had been eliminated or outsourced (the corporate headquarters for US Steel, however, remained downtown). In eight years alone, from 1979 to 1987, the area lost 133,000 industrial jobs. By the dawn of the 1990s, the city of Pittsburgh alone had lost fully a third of its population to economic hemorrhaging.

The full story of what happened in Pittsburgh has never been fully written, or maybe it's more correct to say that it's never been fully learned. What occurred was a tragedy in many ways, but one that's been forgotten, the mills imploded for shopping centers and condominiums built atop riverside gray-slate slag heaps. There is a wound from the collapse, and we don't fully know the language with which to describe it. Perhaps Bruce Springsteen comes closest in his song about the Johnstown Company, "The River," when he asked, "Is a dream a lie if it don't come true? Or is it something worse?" By the end of the millennium, not a single working steel mill remained in Pittsburgh.

AFTERWORD

An East Liberty Parable

During the decades before the American Revolution, a flat area of empty land in a valley several miles east of the forks of the Ohio functioned as what the medieval English had called a "liberty." It functioned as a common grazing ground, whereby people could bring their animals and share in collective stewardship. By the beginning of the nineteenth century, much of the liberty was owned by Alexander Negley, a Swiss-born veteran of the Continental Army who made his fortune from milling. By the time of his passing in 1809, he had one of the largest homes in the area, built of red brick and with orchards spreading out behind it. His son Jacob was the true visionary, for as a speculator, he saw great potential in the former grazing lands. He decided to divide what had been the commons into individual plots. He derived the community's new name from both its former legal status and its direction from the city proper, christening it "East Liberty."

By 1843, Negley was among the richest men in Pittsburgh. That was the year that his daughter would marry an ambitious Ulster Irish lawyer named Thomas Mellon. Dazzled by the opulence of the Negleys' lodgings, Mellon wished to amass his own fortune. He encouraged other wealthy Pittsburghers to move to East Liberty, and as he began to dominate the banking industry, the neighborhood became a leafy respite from downtown smog, especially when a trolley line connected the two neighborhoods. Soon East Liberty began to feature promenades of luxury shops along the former Greensburg Turnpike. Wealthy Pittsburghers from nearby Point Breeze and Shadyside transformed the former commons into a leisure district; its restaurants, shops, and theaters patronized by Carnegie, Heinz, Westinghouse, and Mellon. When the twentieth century began, East Liberty was dotted with rising skyscrapers like the Frick-funded Highland Building, and establishments like the first automobile floor-room, the green-domed Motor Square Garden. East Liberty was the wealthiest business district in the country that wasn't a downtown.

By the time that Thomas's son, Richard Beatty Mellon (brother of Andrew), would fund the construction of the massive gothic cathedral, East Liberty Presbyterian Church, in 1932, the area would be home to more than 50,000 people. Wags called the structure, quickly stained black with mill exhaust, "Mellon's Fire Escape." As a symbol of Protestant ascendancy, the church towered over a surprisingly diverse neighborhood, which was demographically changing by virtue of the train lines that brought people out of the congested inner-city slums. Both ethnically and economically, East Liberty became a diverse microcosm; Italian and Jewish immigrants began to move into the rowhouses on its rectilinear streets, and an influx of Black migrants from the South started to move there in the years before the Depression.

By World War II, banks began using federal census data in a coordinated program of redlining that especially affected Black Pittsburghers. Redlining ensured that the working class were unable to amass the necessary credit required to keep up their homes, and quickly the neighborhood started to segregate. By the 1960s, thousands of residents from the lower Hill were forced into the crowded slums of East Liberty, and in a pique of *noblesse oblige,* the city sponsored the building of massive, dystopian public housing skyscrapers with roads routed directly beneath them, sending plumes of exhaust into residences. Public renewal butchered the grid of the neighborhood, turning its center into a confusing mixture of one-way streets, effectively cutting the community off from the rest of the east end. Through the last decades of the twentieth century, East Liberty was written off as an irredeemable ghetto.

By the turn of the millennium, the roads had been restored and the public housing imploded. Low rents encouraged the opening of trendy restaurants, bars, clubs, galleries, coffee shops, and bookstores, stretching into similarly distressed Garfield. By the time Whole Foods, Starbucks, and Borders moved into East Liberty, the process of gentrification had already marked the neighborhood, as longtime residents were increasingly pushed into the now distressed eastern suburbs that had once been the destination for the white-flight middle class. Soon the short-lived arts community was affected by the demographic changes as well, as rents increased and luxury apartments, condominiums, and hotels began to punctuate the skyline. Massive employers like the University of Pittsburgh Medical Center (long a powerful institution after Jonas Salk cured polio while working as a doctor there in the 1950s) established locations in East Liberty. Two decades after the last steel mill shuttered its doors, this east end neighborhood would become a locus for the tech industry. In 2010, on the site of an abandoned red-bricked factory, which had once been a bakery for the Nabisco Corporation, the tech behemoth Google would open one of their central locations in the United States.

Ten years later, the gentrified neighborhood would become the site of Black Lives Matter protests on behalf of racial justice, a sign that once again, the times were changing. When the results of the 2020 election were announced, Allegheny County's ballots being those that gave former Vice President Joe Biden enough of a lead that he would be awarded Pennsylvania's twenty electoral votes and thus the presidency, Pittsburghers thronged into East Liberty's streets in celebration. Only two years after Pittsburgh had suffered the worst antisemitic massacre in US history in Squirrel

Hill, the city was instrumental in rescuing America from the authoritarianism that had made such violence possible.

East Liberty is Pittsburgh in miniature. Its story is the city's story—from early utopianism, to the fabulous displays of Gilded Age wealth and the aspirations of immigrants arriving to the city, to quixotic urban renewal and decline. And, of course, regeneration (or gentrification, depending on whom you ask). By the new millennium, the population loss stalled, and as the 2010s began, the city slowly increased in size. Unlike other Rust Belt cities, Pittsburgh's economy has always been fairly diverse, and a core of the former aristocracy's money remained in the form of powerful foundations, which played a role in the city weathering its financial storms. The presence of UPMC, the University of Pittsburgh, and Carnegie-Mellon ("meds and eds") was instrumental in the new economy. Major national news outlets extolled the rebirth and Pittsburgh's increasing status as a hipster destination.

Such was the environment when President Barack Obama selected the city for the G20 conference of international leaders in 2009. Postindustrial Pittsburgh traded in its steel for silicon, its iron for apps, and its recovery (for some) was branded as a lesson for a new type of technocratic economics that would ensure a prosperous, progressive, and, most of all, cooler future. Some of this was due, no doubt, to the patience, fortitude, and endurance of Pittsburgh's citizens. Some was due to the foresight of the business and nonprofit communities. And some, of course, was hype. But that begs the question—what is the wisdom in becoming a representative symbol of the neoliberal economic order just as that way of doing things seems as ossified as our previous iteration of industrial capitalism?

Even as Silicon Valley colonizes Pittsburgh, some of the old proletarian fire remains. In 2019, tech contractors at Google voted to unionize. They joined the United Steelworkers. Such is the nature of our identity, especially for those of us born in the midst of the devouring, tethered to something we only have the dimmest memories of. Any number of hypotheses can be proffered for what made Pittsburgh so successful in the first place; any number formulated to explain why the city has recovered. A geologist can give you recourse to the veins of coal which once threaded the earth; a geographer can place it within a network of rivers linking east to west. Historians will examine how the ethos of the frontier changed into the optimism of industrialization, and demographers will celebrate the city's diversity. Pittsburghers, no doubt, will extol the unique grit of the people themselves.

All of these are partially true, but the reality is, I think, something all the simpler and yet more mysterious. For it must be admitted that the place is almost preternaturally charged with a broken beauty, a tinge of the numinous throughout the landscape itself. From the moment the first people arrived in these hills, they couldn't have helped but sense that which the English novelist D. H. Lawrence called the "spirit of place," and it will still endure even after the lights cascading down the hills like molten steel have gone out. There is something transcendental about how the rivers wind and cut through the green-robed mountains, the manner in which the valleys descend deep into the earth and the hills puncture the horizon like the planet's spine. When visitors emerge from the Fort Pitt tunnel into the dazzling birth of lights that is Pittsburgh, they are almost always struck by the sheer, incandescent beauty of the place.

Through it all, despite it all, enduring through it all, that has been the constant—the holy, strange, sacred, withering sublimity of the landscape itself. Long after whatever is to come, whether the lights turn out in the skyscrapers and the banks of the rivers themselves explode, or if some better, newer, freer world should emerge, this place will still ultimately always have that same quality, that constant spirit of place. This has always been the secret of its endurance, this has always been the reason for its emergence, its resurrection. For regardless of what happens or what will happen, there is a wisdom in knowing that this place—this Pittsburgh—is beautiful.

9 781948 742924